# JAMES AGEE
## Reconsiderations

Tennessee Studies in Literature Volume 33

JAMES AGEE

*Reconsiderations*

*Edited by Michael A. Lofaro*

THE UNIVERSITY OF TENNESSEE PRESS / KNOXVILLE

TENNESSEE STUDIES IN LITERATURE

Editorial Board: Don R. Cox, Allison R. Ensor, Richard J. Finneran,
Nancy M. Goslee, R. Baxter Miller, Norman J. Sanders

"Tennessee Studies in Literature," a distinguished series sponsored by the Department of English at The University of Tennessee, Knoxville, began publication in 1956. Beginning in 1984, with Volume 27, TSL evolved from a series of annual volumes of miscellaneous essays to a series of occasional volumes, each one dealing with a specific theme, period, or genre, for which the editor of that volume has invited contributions from leading scholars in the field.

Inquiries concerning this series should be addressed to the Editorial Board, Tennessee Studies in Literature, Department of English, The University of Tennessee, Knoxville, Tennessee 37996-0430. Those desiring to purchase additional copies of this issue or copies of back issues should address The University of Tennessee Press, 293 Communications Building, Knoxville, Tennessee 37996-0325.

Frontispiece: Portrait of James Agee commissioned for the East Tennessee Hall of Fame for the Performing Arts housed in the historic Bijou Theater in Knoxville. Artist A. Lee Lively, c/o Portrait's South, 515 North Bragg, Lookout Mountain, TN 37350.

**Library of Congress Cataloging in Publication Data**

James Agee : reconsiderations / edited by Michael A. Lofaro. — 1st ed.
    p.  cm. — (Tennessee studies in literature ; v. 33)
   Includes bibliographical references and index.
   ISBN 0-87049-756-1 (cloth: alk. paper)
   1. Agee, James, 1909-1955—Criticism and interpretation.
  I. Lofaro, Michael A., 1948-  . II. Series
  PS3501.G35Z736 1992
  818'.5209—dc20             92-1405
                   CIP

*For Helen Wasson Lofaro*

# Contents

I've thought of inventing a sort of amphibious style—prose that would run into poetry when the occasion demanded poetic expression. That may be the solution; but I don't entirely like the idea. What I want to do is, to devise a poetic diction that will cover the whole range of events as perfectly and evenly as skin covers every organ, vital as well as trivial, of the human body.

—*James Agee to Father Flye*
*[Cambridge, Mass.] November 19, 1930*

I truly have not any doubt but very strongly the opposite of the balances, some of them clear and positive, and others mysterious, that there are in existence, and it is their interlocking or fusion with "evil" that may be, next to the plain effort to contemplate, the chief "fascination" or binding-into-living; and I'm very much more drawn toward innocence, and the relaxed or abandoned brain, and simplicity and childhood, and the so called "sub"-human for that matter and "sub"-organic, than I've appeared by the ways I've written; but I'm also interested in finding how qualified, luke-warm at heart, and corrupted so many of the balancers are, and in the idea that nothing does quite so much harm or evil as innocence or guiltlessness which is so innocent it doesn't see the traps and its double or triple meanings.

—*James Agee to Father Flye*
*[Frenchtown, New Jersey, September 16, 1938]*

# Preface

*Michael A. Lofaro*

ANY REEVALUATION of the work of James Agee must deal with the man himself. So complex, so diverse, and so driven was Agee that he seemed a sometimes willing and sometimes reluctant participant in the issues and debates that sought to define the relationship of life, literature, and art to the creative process in the modern age. The significance of his accomplishments has been overshadowed by his short, turbulent, sprawling, and introspective life, which revealed him to be an egocentric individual who was both intellectually self-absorbed and physically self-consuming. Further distraction has resulted from the breadth of his writing—his poetry, fiction, nonfiction, journalism, film reviews, and screenplays—an expansive scope that left him open to the charge of never perfecting his talents in a single area.

Several of the critics whose essays make up this volume argue persuasively that far more literary and artistic recognition is due to Agee than is usually granted. Taken as a whole, these analyses demonstrate Agee's lifelong participation in one of the central debates of modern aesthetics and how profound an effect this debate had on the literature that he produced. They also show that James Agee was unquestionably preoccupied with a sense of place that was ingrained in him in boyhood. He then tested the temper of his fiery creative process against his Knoxville, Tennessee, heritage and his evolving personal, religious, and political beliefs by becoming immersed in and often obsessed by the possibilities and impossibilities of reconciling the Romantic and Modern viewpoints. His struggle over the decision between perfecting his life or his art was made all the more poignant by a substantial flowering of the best and worst of the Industrial Age in a growing city with firmly planted agrarian roots and by his subsequent education in the bucolic and contemplative setting of St. Andrew's School near Sewanee, Tennessee.

Against these experiences and the broadening background of his student years at Phillips Exeter Academy and Harvard and his work as a writer in New York and Hollywood, Agee's life developed into a near-classic case study of the dilemma of the twentieth-century artist. His art was clearly the result of a painful and dynamic tension that he fought to control. In a June 28, 1938, letter to his lifelong friend and confidant Father Flye, Agee noted that:

> Quite plainly I know that in the most important things, or many of them, in my existence, I cannot know for sure what I am doing, or why, or at all surely the difference between right and wrong, which latter very often appear to be identical or so interlocked that destruction of one entails the destruction of the other, like separating Siamese twins who use the same heart and bloodstream. This may simply mean that he who moves beyond the safety of the rules finds himself inevitably in the "tragedy" of the "human situation," which rules have been built to avoid or anaesthetize, and which must be undertaken without anaesthetic: but I am suspicious of laying pity and grief and sadness to such a general, fatal source rather than to a source for which I am personally responsible.[1]

Such existential acceptance, however, neither resolved the tension nor allowed Agee to dissolve the barriers between life and art. In the "Preamble" to *Let Us Now Praise Famous Men*, he used an analogy to music to underscore his belief that transcendence could at best only be approached, not completely attained.

> Get a radio or phonograph capable of the most extreme loudness possible, and sit down to listen to a performance of Beethoven's Seventh Symphony or of Schubert's C-Major Symphony. But I don't mean just sit down and listen. I mean this: Turn it on as loud as you can get it. Then get down on the floor and jam your ear as close into

the loudspeaker as you can get it and stay there, breathing as lightly as possible, and not moving, and neither eating nor smoking nor drinking. Concentrate everything you can into your hearing and into your body. You won't hear it nicely. If it hurts you, be glad of it. *As near as you will ever get* [emphasis added], you are inside the music; not only inside it, you are it; your body is no longer your shape and substance, it is the shape and substance of the music.[2]

This total apprehension of what Agee had earlier termed "the cruel radiance of what is" was part of his experimental nature and part of his quest toward a "whole of consciousness" in which "in the immediate world, everything is to be discerned, for him who can discern it, and centrally and simply, without either dissection into science, or digestion into art."[3]

But the price of attempting transcendent wholeness was high. At times Agee ravaged his own life, seemingly all too ready to follow Walter Pater's admonition to artists of the late Victorian era to burn with a hard gemlike flame in their writing; and he, like many of those of the fin-de-siècle era, made it a model for life as well. At other times, his gusto and limitless vitality were singularly converted into unique, innovative works like the audacious and uncategorizable *Let Us Now Praise Famous Men*, which revealed an undeniable bond between Agee and the Alabama tenant families who were his ostensible subject, and the highly charged autobiographical fiction of *A Death in the Family*, which vividly detailed the unfolding trauma of his father's death in a highly poetic prose.

This volume focuses upon these two major works and upon Agee's explorations of the possibilities and limitations of narrative technique to highlight his literary achievements and their regional, national, and international appeal. It also demonstrates that the measure of their success is in large part the direct result of his supposed flaws, his variety of subject and form and his life of often reckless abandon.

## Notes

1.  *Letters of James Agee to Father Flye* (New York: Braziller, 1962), 101.
2.  James Agee and Walker Evans, *Let Us Now Praise Famous Men* (1941; rpt. Boston: Houghton, 1988), 15–16.
3.  Ibid., 11.

# Editor's Note

THE READER MAY WELL be puzzled in regard to an apparent discrepancy in this volume concerning the title of James Agee's "Knoxville: Summer of 1915." Agee originally completed the piece in 1935, and it was published with that title in the *Partisan Review* in 1938; Samuel Barber's 1948 musical composition based on Agee's work was also entitled "Knoxville: Summer of 1915" but added the subtitle "For Voice and Orchestra"; and when David McDowell edited Agee's manuscript of *A Death in the Family* for publication in 1957, he incorporated the work into the text with the title "Knoxville: Summer 1915." These small distinctions are retained in this volume. An errant comma was introduced ("Knoxville: Summer, 1915") in the chapter title of the frequently reprinted Bantam paperback edition, but not in its Table of Contents. This same title sometimes appeared on the record jacket of Barber's composition.

# Acknowledgments

I SHOULD LIKE to thank all those people who have aided and encouraged the preparation of this volume, but especially my wife Nancy and my children, Ellen and Christopher, who provided the time necessary to complete it. I should also like to thank the members of the editorial board of *Tennessee Studies in Literature* and the trustees of the Better English Fund established by the late Dr. John C. Hodges for the Department of English of the University of Tennessee for their kind and generous support, and Ms. Sandra Groves Hancock for her assistance in preparing the index.

# Introduction:
# The Agee Legacy

*Wilma Dykeman*

IN A COMFORTABLE, old, Victorian house in a middle-class neighborhood of Knoxville, Tennessee, James Agee spent his childhood. But words such as *comfortable, middle-class,* and *spent* seem oddly inappropriate when associated with James Agee. This was a man whose raw sensitivity to the awesome condition of being human stretched him on a lifelong rack between anguish and exultation, rage and love. Nothing comfortable. This was a human being who looked at all other humans with a compassion that knew neither class nor any other artificial distinctions. And even in childhood this was an artist whose time was not spent but absorbed, devoured through the senses of the flesh and subtleties of the intellect. In short, James Agee was proof of Emerson's statement, "Talent alone is not enough. There must be a man behind the book."

In March of 1989 the University of Tennessee at Knoxville honored this native son and itself with a wide-ranging quest of "The Agee Legacy." At that time I wrote:

> It is the man and his books, inseparable, we would honor this week in Knoxville, Tennessee. An occasion long overdue.
> But (to search even as he might for a true and worthy meaning) is the word *honor*—a stately, remote, disembodied word—appropriate for James Agee? Would *celebrate* be better? Or has that word been trivialized beyond recognition to a shallow, commercialized event

reaching no deeper than the skin, no farther than the moment—or week?

Perhaps we should say only that we set aside an interval of time to refresh and improve understanding of a person who struggled to be as large as life, whose talent was sometimes larger than life.

James Agee's vitality and the variety of his writing continue to astonish and challenge us. This week we shall renew acquaintance with the times in which he lived and worked; we shall rediscover a few of the many voices by which he sought to awaken us to the riches and paradoxes and terror of being human. His legacy is in novels and poems and short stories, journalism and films and film criticism and social commentary. Our main focus will be on that unique achievement, *Let Us Now Praise Famous Men*. At the age of fifty, it remains both timely and timeless.

We hope that James Rufus Agee would look kindly on a university, a Knoxville effort, to talk now of an uncommonly attentive human being who once lived here, successfully disguised to himself as a child.

The bounty of Agee's creativity presented both a blessing and a problem for those arranging the program to fill that week. (Earlier versions of some of the essays gathered here were presented during the week of "The Agee Legacy.") The audience, it was hoped, would be drawn not only from academic ranks but from a wider community as well. Intellectual discussion could provide an important context for rereading Agee's work and fresh evaluation of its role in American cultural history. More personal interpretations and insights would quicken awareness of his voice as it spoke to a new generation of readers, those unacquainted with his work, or, as in the case of his films, those acquainted with certain classics but unaware that Agee was their author.

Obviously, choices were to be made between addressing the breadth or the depth of Agee's writing. A career that began with publication of an acclaimed volume of poems and ended with a posthumous Pulitzer Prize–winning novel is impressive. But sandwich between these two communiqués from a tortured, searching talent an outpouring of articles for the nation's leading journals, another novel, short stories, book reviews, film criticism which granted movies the dignity of art, television and screen plays, and extraordinary letters to a friend and mentor, and we have—well, as the disembodied voices of the three-ring Ringling, Barnum and Bailey performances used to say, "the one, the only, the original" James Rufus Agee. Agee it was and is, spying out the details of our days, observing the circus of our lives, passionately intent on capturing it all precisely and completely—in words.

*Let Us Now Praise Famous Men* was chosen as a centerpiece for the week with Agee. To provide a broader background than could be presented at the conference, Kathryn Black Swain now gives an overview of Agee's achievements with a chronology of events and a brief biography of the author. George Brown Tindall was the happy choice to open the actual program series with a historical context for the visit that Agee and photographer Walker Evans made to three tenant families in Alabama. "The Lost World of Agee's *Let Us Now Praise Famous Men*" reconstructs the South as it was during the era of cotton tenancy and especially the decade of the 1930s.

Drawing on his extensive scholarship relating to this period, Tindall provides a view of the rural world Agee and Evans entered in the South of 1936. Given the character of these two young seers, their assignment was doomed to failure as a piece of journalism, and later to "fail" on its initial publication as a book. Eventual resurrection of *Let Us Now Praise Famous Men* as an American classic has kept the "lost world" so ably defined by Tindall alive in the American consciousness, if not so clearly quick in its conscience.

Following the historical background for *Let Us Now Praise Famous Men*, David Madden effectively probes the tensions and paradoxes of Agee's personality and prose, especially as they shaped creation of a book under the "compulsion to transcend both the journalistic assignment and his own artistic aspirations." In his "The Test of a First-Rate Intelligence: Agee and the Cruel Radiance of What Is," Madden also compares Agee's work with that of other American writers, especially several of his contemporaries. Finally, Madden poses the question of failure. His argument is persuasive: "What Agee could not do, Time has done for him, brought into harmony the conflicting elements in *Famous Men*." The result is "What many readers would testify, that it is the great prose lyric of American literature."

Linda Wagner-Martin presents another frame of vision in "*Let Us Now Praise Famous Men*—and Women: Agee's Absorption in the

Sexual." Her close reading of the text and freshly related insights bear out her theme that a "sense of the plausibility of love, of caring both sexual and asexual, suffuses Agee's text." Joining other contributors to this volume in acknowledging the uniqueness of Agee's work, Wagner-Martin discovers that the "distinctions he appears to establish" between the outer, "intellectualized matter" and the inner "seminal core of human life" are "finally, false. Rather than a boxlike structure, Agee's house of fiction becomes a vortex, a single center of focus."

Agee's journalism is sometimes deplored as a detour deflecting him from the high road of art. Paul Ashdown's "Prophet from Highland Avenue: James Agee's Visionary Journalism" is a compelling portrait of the artist as twentieth-century journalist/prophet. Invoking a genre that reaches from eminent Victorians to some of our own chic contemporaries, Ashdown argues that Agee's magazine articles incorporated "monstrous intuitions and strange prophecies" that fulfilled at least one scholar's "criteria for the twentieth-century sage." Add the intense personal awareness, memories, and sensory details that characterized Agee's "commercial work," and the result is inimitable and powerful. Ashdown's insights and well-chosen quotations on subjects reaching from the atomic bomb to a television script on "Abraham Lincoln—The Early years" and, finally, Agee's commentary on Chaplin's *City Lights*, in which "the Tramp causes a blind girl to regain her sight," refresh our sense of Agee's enduring voice of prophecy. It is a voice Biblical in its wrath toward all that would destroy or fail to see the "shining joy" in the face of the little Tramp as he gave "sight to the blind."

Agee's "cinematic eye and musical ear" as essential to the creation of a unified vision of himself, his fellow man, all of creation and his God" shape Eugene T. Carroll's discussion of "Mood and Music: Landscape and Artistry in *A Death in the Family*." "Knoxville: Summer 1915," which opens the novel, a "creative musical experience," was, indeed, set to music by the American composer Samuel Barber in 1947. Carroll gives it close attention as a tone poem. He accords similar scrutiny to the novel's interlaced "music and mood to conceptualize the unity of ploy, setting, characters and themes." There is special appreciation for Agee's effort to address "the universal questions of life, death and resurrection," while many of his contemporaries "were writing of man's alienation from his fellow man and the deficiencies of human nature."

"Urban and Rural Balance in *A Death in the Family*" presents Victor A. Kramer with the opportunity to explore Agee's fictional evocation of the "country-city conflict central to American experience from post–Civil War days into the present." That conflict is a basic tension among the well-loved, very human characters in the quiet, unfolding family drama of the novel. *A Death in the Family*, "a very private book," draws on Agee's own experience, as proved by the many unpublished notes and reflections Kramer has drawn upon for a rich background to the composition of the novel. It also becomes "a picture of a particular era when urban and rural were blended." In specific quotations and careful juxtaposition of materials used and unused in the final version of the novel, Kramer leads us to appreciate and share Agee's reach for "the universal by means of a careful rendition of the particular."

"James Agee: A Bibliography of Secondary Sources," by Mary Moss, confirms the "enduring power" of Agee's work. The present volume may now be added to that bibliography. Perhaps each of the contributors, struggling toward understanding of Agee's words, struggling to communicate the frustration and fullness of that understanding, shared Agee's own "compulsion to transcend both the journalistic assignment and his [her] own artistic aspirations."

That is as it should be. Agee did not leave tidy answers. His legacy is the questions, the search, wrenching us from the oblivion of trivial diversions to a painful and joyous reality of our barbaric and divine humanity.

# An Agee Chronology

## Kathryn Black Swain

1909    *Nov. 27.* James Rufus Agee is born to Laura Tyler Agee
        and Hugh James Agee in Knoxville, Tennessee.

1916    *May 18.* Hugh James Agee is killed instantly when he
        drives his car off the road.

1919    *Fall.* Laura Tyler Agee and her two children, Rufus and
        Emma, move to the campus of St. Andrew's School near
        Sewanee, Tennessee, where Rufus is enrolled. There he
        meets Father Flye, who remains a lifelong friend.

1924    Agee returns to Knoxville to attend Knoxville High
        School. His mother marries Father Erskine Wright and
        moves with him to Rockland, Maine.

1925    *Summer.* Agee travels to France and England with Father
        Flye.

        *Fall.* Agee enters Phillips Exeter Academy in Exeter, New
        Hampshire.

1927    Agee is elected editor of Exeter's *Monthly* and president of Exeter's literary Lantern Club.

1928    *Fall.* Agee is accepted at Harvard, where he is quickly accepted by the literary set.

1929    *Summer.* Agee spends the summer as a migrant farm worker and hobo in Nebraska and Kansas.

1931    *Spring.* Agee is elected president of the *Harvard Advocate.*

1932    *Mar. 18.* The *Advocate's* parody of *Time,* prepared under Agee's leadership, is published.

        Agee graduates from Harvard and gets a job at *Fortune* with the assistance of Dwight Macdonald, a Phillips Exeter alumnus.

1933    *Jan. 28.* Marries Olivia Saunders, the daughter of Professor Percy Saunders and Louise Saunders. Agee had been introduced to the Saunders family by one of his Harvard professors, and Louise Saunders became a surrogate mother to him and was his closest confidante for several years.

1934    *Fall.* With the assistance and encouragement of Archibald MacLeish, Agee submits *Permit Me Voyage,* a collection of poems, to the Yale Series of Younger Poets, and it is accepted for publication.

1935    *Nov. to May 1936.* On leave from *Fortune,* Agee spends almost six months living and writing in Anna Maria, Florida, where he completes "Knoxville: Summer of 1915," published in the *Partisan Review* in 1938, and works on *A Death in the Family.*

1936 *Summer.* In June, Agee receives a *Fortune* assignment to investigate the predicament of the tenant farmer; he and photographer Walker Evans live with a tenant family for several weeks.

1937 Agee begins an affair with Alma Mailman, an acquaintance of the Saunders family.

 *Summer.* Agee gives up his staff position at *Fortune* and begins free-lancing for the magazine.

1938 *Nov.* Agee's divorce from Olivia Saunders is final.

 *Dec. 6.* Agee marries Alma Mailman, his mistress.

1939 *Spring.* Agee discontinues his association with *Fortune.*

 *Summer. Harper's* rejects "Three Tenant Families."

 *Fall.* Robert Fitzgerald offers Agee a job reviewing books for *Time.*

1940 Agee begins an affair with Mia Fritsch, a researcher at *Fortune.*

 *Mar. 20.* Alma gives birth to Agee's first son, Joel.

 *Winter.* Alma leaves Agee, taking Joel with her to Mexico.

1941 *Fall.* After extended hesitation and negotiation, Houghton Mifflin publishes *Let Us Now Praise Famous Men* to mixed reviews and dismal sales.

 Agee begins reviewing films for *Time.*

1942 *Dec. 26.* Agee begins reviewing films for *The Nation;* he continues there until September 4, 1948.

1944     *July 30.* Mia Fritsch gives birth prematurely to a son who dies shortly afterwards.

         *Fall.* Agee marries Mia Fritsch.

1945     *Fall.* Agee begins writing special feature stories for *Time*.

1946     *Nov. 7.* Julia Teresa, Agee's first daughter, is born.

1948     *Apr. 9.* American composer Samuel Barber's "Knoxville: Summer of 1915," a composition "For Voice and Orchestra" based on Agee's prose poem of the same title, premieres in Boston.

         *Aug. 30.* Agee leaves *Time*.

         *Sept. 4.* Agee's final assignment for *The Nation* appears.

         Huntington Hartford hires Agee to write a screen adaptation of Stephen Crane's short story, "The Blue Hotel."

1949     *Feb. 13. The Quiet One*, a film about Wiltwyck, a school for delinquent children, opens in New York City to rave reviews. This product of collaboration between Agee and photographer Helen Levitt later wins the Venice film Festival's Best film award.

         *Sept. 3.* "Comedy's Greatest Era," Agee's article on silent movies, is published in *Life*.

1950     *May 15.* Andrea Maria, Agee's second daughter, is born.

         *Sept. 18.* "Undirectable Director," Agee's article on John Huston, is published in *Life*.

*Fall.* John Huston hires Agee to come to California to write a screenplay based on C. S. Forester's novel, *The African Queen.*

1951    *Jan. 15.* Agee suffers his first major heart attack and is hospitalized for several weeks; Huston must write the conclusion of *The African Queen.*

*Apr.* Houghton Mifflin publishes *The Morning Watch,* a short novel based on Agee's years at St. Andrew's.

1952    *Apr. 22.* Agee is commissioned by the Ford Foundation to write a television script about Abraham Lincoln.

*Winter.* Agee writes the screenplay for another Huntington Hartford production of a Stephen Crane short story, "The Bride Comes to Yellow Sky."

1953    Agee writes the screenplay *Noa Noa,* based on Paul Gauguin's diary.

1954    Agee is hired by actor Charles Laughton to write a screenplay based on Davis Grubb's novel, *The Night of the Hunter.* Agee's screenplay is rejected by Laughton, who writes the script actually used for the movie.

*Sept. 6.* John Alexander, Agee's second son, is born.

1955    *May 16.* Agee suffers his final heart attack and dies in a taxi in New York City on the way to his doctor's office.

1957    *A Death in the Family* is edited by David McDowell and published posthumously by McDowell, Obolensky.

1958    Agee is posthumously awarded the Pulitzer Prize for his novel *A Death in the Family.*

McDowell, Obolensky publishes *Agee on Film: Reviews and Comments,* volume 1, a collection of Agee's film reviews and articles on movies.

1960    McDowell, Obolensky publishes *Agee on Film: Five Film Scripts by James Agee,* volume 2, which includes Agee's screenplays, *Noa Noa, The African Queen, The Bride Comes to Yellow Sky,* and *The Blue Hotel,* and Laughton's script for *The Night of the Hunter.*

Houghton Mifflin reissues *Let Us Now Praise Famous Men.*

*Nov. 30.* Tad Mosel's stage adaptation of *A Death in the Family* opens on Broadway. This play, entitled *All the Way Home,* is awarded a Pulitzer Prize and a Drama Critics' Award.

1962    *The Letters of James Agee to Father Flye* published by George Braziller.

1963    *Fall.* The screen version of *All the Way Home,* starring Jean Simmons and Robert Preston, premiers in Knoxville.

1968    *The Collected Poems of James Agee* and *The Collected Short Prose of James Agee,* both edited by Robert Fitzgerald, are published by Houghton Mifflin.

1988    Houghton Mifflin reissues *Let Us Now Praise Famous Men* with an introduction by John Hersey.

# Agee: A Brief Life

## Kathryn Black Swain

KNOXVILLE: SUMMER 1991. On Highland Avenue, many of the Victorian houses James Agee described in "Knoxville: Summer of 1915" still stand gazing into each others' windows. Most of them have endured the humiliations of old age and neglect, but, even leaning at odd angles and wearing peeling and oddly colored coats of paint, they exhibit a hard-earned grace. This is no longer a neighborhood of families. Rarely will a six-year-old boy be seen lounging in the grass or strolling with his father. The occupants of these humbled houses, now divided into drafty apartments, are students, young men and women attending the University of Tennessee lying only a few blocks away. Even those who are fortunate enough to live in the new condominiums built on the site of Agee's home are almost certainly unaware that a child named Rufus was born here, came to consciousness here, lost his father here, and left something here that he could never recover.

Highland Avenue has changed, but when James Agee wrote "Knoxville: Summer of 1915," which became the prologue for *A Death in the Family*, he was not writing about a place but about the brief and long-lost equilibrium of his childhood—a delicate balance that was permanently upset by his father's death; and he wrote from the perspective of a man who had long searched unsuccessfully for some way back to the harmony and security this place came to represent. That the neighborhood where Agee was born is filled with students engaged in similar quests for security, belonging, and self-esteem seems an appropriate tribute to the man who carried within him all his life memories of this place, if not the tranquility it symbolized.

*A Death in the Family*, Agee's long-planned memorial to his father, commemorates both his tranquil childhood and the tragic event that accelerated his loss of innocence and security—the death of his father, Hugh James (Jay) Agee. If the childhood Agee depicts in the novel is not perfectly serene,[1] the life after Jay's death, as represented in the novel, in James Agee's letters and journals, and in discussions by friends and biographers, seems to have been almost devoid of serenity. Whether the result of a natural bent or of Jay Agee's death and its aftermath, recurrent depression plagued James Agee for the rest of his life.[2] His major weapons in the struggle with "melancholia"—work, romantic love, and alcohol—often seem to have amplified his pain.

It has been said that Jay Agee's death was the central experience of his son's childhood,[3] and *A Death in the Family* is the proof of the immediate and long-term effects of Jay's death. In the novel, Agee describes his childhood as generally quite comfortable and secure, although there was some conflict between his parents. In addition to differences in education and social class, his parents (represented by Jay and Mary) possessed opposing character traits. Laura Whitman Tyler Agee was a devout Anglo-Catholic. Though Jay respected Laura's wishes to raise their children in her faith, he was not a religious man. Laura's strict religious beliefs made her seem stern while Jay's jovial, warm personality, unhampered by religious strictures, made him seem affectionate and tolerant. In spite of the inevitable friction caused by his parents' contrasting temperaments, James Agee remembered the earliest years of his childhood as idyllic. Jay Agee's good cheer generally held sway over Laura's serious nature, and young Rufus, as James was then called, enjoyed a relatively carefree life surrounded by a loving extended family and basking in the affection of the father he idolized.

This idyllic period came to an end on May 18, 1916, as Jay Agee was killed instantly when his car went off the road after an overnight emergency visit to his ill father. The title of *A Death in the Family* refers not just to Jay Agee's death but to what seemed to young Rufus to be the dissolution of the family. The loss of the love and guidance of his father was followed by removal from the tightly knit circle of extended family that had surrounded him in Knoxville. Three years after Jay's death, Laura Agee moved with James and his sister, Emma, to St. Andrew's School near Sewanee, Tennessee, where she felt that her son would benefit from masculine role models and receive a strong religious grounding. Although Agee maintained contact with the Tylers all his life, the move from Knoxville deprived him of the accustomed constant attention and affection of his mother's family. In addition, Laura Agee's conviction that her son needed masculine influence led her to restrict his visits with her to once a week.[4] For young James, the move to St. Andrews intensified the painful feelings of isolation that had begun with his father's death.

Deprived of a normal family life, James Agee made education the center of his life from that first autumn at St. Andrews in 1919 until his graduation from Harvard in 1932. While he was at St. Andrews, the boy threw himself into his studies and was perceived as exceptionally intelligent by both teachers and fellow students. It was also at St. Andrews that Agee began his lifelong friendship with Father James Flye, one of the teachers there. In Father Flye, Agee found the almost unconditional love and emotional support that he so desperately needed. The priest shared many of the child's interests and spent many hours with the boy discussing such topics as nature, literature, and religion. Flye himself denied that he served as a surrogate father to young Rufus;[5] it is undeniable, however, that the boy responded quite positively to the support and attention of the priest, who was only a little younger than Jay Agee had been when he died. The regular correspondence between Agee and Father Flye, which continued throughout Agee's life, attests to the strength of this early bond.

Although Agee had enjoyed his academic pursuits at St. Andrews, it was not until he attended Phillips Exeter Academy, a prestigious preparatory school in New Hampshire, that he conceived the desire to become a great writer. It was here that Agee finally dropped the name Rufus, which he had never liked, and chose to be called James or Jim. His overall grades at Exeter were unpredictable, but his performance in literature and composition courses was consistently excellent; he won several literary honors and edited and frequently contributed to the *Phillips Exeter Monthly,* demonstrating early in his writing career his propensity for experimentation in different genres such as lyric and narrative poetry, prose and verse drama, short fiction, essays, and translations.

Agee's literary development continued at Harvard, where he entered as a freshman in 1928. He was once again quickly accepted in literary circles and in 1931 was made editor of the *Harvard Advocate.* As at Exeter, he continued to contribute works of his own in different genres, taking advantage of the intellectual and literary atmosphere to experiment further with new forms and methods. The drastic mood swings that had first appeared at Phillips Exeter also continued. Agee's self-confidence spurred his belief in his potential as a writer, but the self-deprecation that had always caused him to devalue his abilities made his goals seem unachievable. In November of 1930, he wrote to Father Flye:

> I'm from now on committed to writing with a horrible definiteness.
> In fact it amounts to a rather unhealthy obsession. . . . The thing I'm trying hardest to do is, to decide what I want to write, and in exactly what way. . . . The great trouble is, I'm terribly anxious to do as well as I possibly can. It sounds conceited; whether it is or not: I'd do anything on earth to become a really great writer. . . . Do you see though, where it leads me? In the first place I have no faith to speak of in my native ability to become more than a very minor writer. My intellectual pelvic girdle simply is not Miltonically wide.[6]

In spite of his insecurity, Agee continued to write. During his last year at Harvard, as editor of the *Advocate,* Agee presided over the preparation of a highly successful parody of *Time* magazine that became his passport to a journalistic career.

In 1932, based on the success of the *Time* parody and on the recommendation of Dwight Macdonald, the Exeter alumnus with whom Agee had corresponded since his Exeter days, Agee was hired as a reporter for *Fortune* magazine. Agee was initially delighted and grateful to land such a position in the midst of the Great Depression, but Macdonald was quick to point out that the work at the magazine would not nurture Agee's creative writing.[7] Agee found far less time available to work on his poetry and fiction than he needed. Convinced that "there is no job on earth that is not bad for the writer; including writing,"[8] Agee was, nevertheless, unable to discover an alternative to magazine writing. For sixteen years after graduating from Harvard, Agee was primarily a magazine writer, serving variously as staff writer for *Fortune*, book reviewer, then film reviewer for *Time*, and film critic for *The Nation*.

Many critics blame Agee's magazine work for his low literary output, and it is true that during this period, if one discounts his often unsigned *Fortune* articles and the numerous film reviews, Agee's published "literary" works number only two: *Permit Me Voyage* (1934), a collection of poems, and *Let Us Now Praise Famous Men* (1941), a collaborative work with photographer Walker Evans that was developed from a *Fortune* assignment. But it may be a mistake to believe that Agee might have produced more literature if he had had more time. As Kenneth Seib has pointed out, Agee actually needed discipline far more than freedom. He was an obsessive rewriter plagued with chronic self-doubt, and his journalistic employment, with the discipline of the deadline, may actually have stimulated more work than it stymied.[9]

The need to write assigned articles and reviews in order to earn a living and the insecurity that triggered endless revisions were not the only factors that interfered with James Agee's literary output. A secure and stable marriage might have allayed his insecurities and restored some of the lost childhood tranquility, but Agee could not sustain such a marriage. In romance, as in talent and creative energy, Agee's problem was not poverty but an embarrassment of riches. There were always women who were willing to attempt to fulfill the handsome and appealing Agee's needs and desires, but Agee was seldom contented with one woman for long. Each love was marked by an almost adolescent adoration and little emotional restraint. And in typically paradoxical fashion, Agee seldom fell quite out of love with any woman, even when he was in the throes of a new romance. Agee tormented himself and the women he loved through protracted periods of hesitation and emotional see-sawing.

On January 28, 1933, Agee married Olivia Saunders, the daughter of Professor Percy Saunders and his wife, Louise. The Saunders family had served as a surrogate family for Agee, and his respect for them and desire to secure himself a place among them almost certainly increased his attraction to their daughter, Olivia, "Via" Saunders.[10] Whether he was ever actually in love with Via or merely convinced himself that he was, he took his marriage seriously and was filled with remorse and regret when he saw that his attachment to Via was not sufficiently strong to sustain it.

Agee's devotion to the Saunders family and his shame over the disintegration of his marriage did not prevent him from starting an affair with Alma Mailman, a friend of the Saunders family. Still, he was unable to choose between the two women and even expressed to Father Flye the desire to be married to both at once.[11] By the time Agee actually gathered the courage to make the split final, everyone else had apparently accepted the inevitable. Early in 1938, Agee and Alma moved together to Frenchtown, New Jersey. By the end of the year, they were married.[12]

The second marriage was briefer than the first. Sometime in 1940, after *Harper's* rejection of "Three Tenant Families," the work that would evolve into *Let Us Now Praise Famous Men*, and during Alma's pregnancy with his first son, Agee initiated another affair, this time with Mia Fritsch, a researcher at *Fortune*. In the winter of 1940, Alma left Agee, taking their infant son, Joel, with her.[13]

The two failed marriages did give Agee some insight into his susceptibility to sexual enticement and the havoc that such philandering and its concomitant emotional upheavals could wreak on his work. In 1941, a disillusioned James Agee wrote:

> I am thirty-one now, and I can conceivably forgive myself my last ten years only by a devotion to work in the next ten which I suspect I'll be incapable of. I am much too vulnerable to human relationships, particularly sexual or in any case heterosexual, and much too deeply wrought upon by them, and in turn much too dependent in my work on feeling, as against "intellect." In short I'm easily upset and, when upset, incapable of decent work. . . . I must learn my way in an exceedingly quiet marriage (which can be wonderful I've found but is basically not at all my style or apparent "nature") or break from marriage and all close liaisons altogether and learn how to live alone & keep love at a bearable distance.[14]

Agee was never able to "keep love at a bearable distance." In fall of 1944, he joined Mia Fritsch in what was to be his nearest approach to a "quiet marriage."

This time, neither Agee nor his lover was in any hurry to marry. When the ceremony did take place, it was instigated by Agee's growing respect and admiration for Mia rather than by pressure from her or society at large. Mia was a strong and independent woman who was undoubtedly more psychologically and emotionally suited to deal with Agee than either of his previous wives had been. His intellectual equal, she was better able to appreciate his genius and to understand the difficulties of his occupation. The period from about 1940 to 1950, before Agee went to Hollywood to work for John Huston, was a time during which he was able to focus much of his energy on his own work. It is during this period that Agee completed *The Morning Watch* (1951) and substantially completed *A Death in the Family*, published posthumously in 1957. Unfortunately, neither Mia's acceptance and love nor Agee's dynamism and determination could shield him from the long-term effects of his habits of excess.

Throughout his school years and his early years in New York, Agee had drawn on an apparently boundless reserve of energy. His determination to succeed, combined with his self-doubt, drove him to invest inordinate effort in every assignment. As he aged, Agee's general carelessness with his health degenerated into outright self-destructiveness. According to Mia, "he was psychologically incapable of moderation, even during the period of his last illness. His motto was 'a little bit too much is just enough for me.'"[15] Agee had always been susceptible to depression, and, as he approached the age at which his father had died, melancholia gave way to a conviction that he, too, would die at thirty-six.[16] His drinking, smoking, overwork, and extramarital liaisons were rapidly eroding his health, and he could not exert sufficient control over these habits to diminish the deterioration.

Agee's 1951–52 trip to Hollywood, during which he produced most of the screenplay for *The African Queen*, marks the end of what he perceived as enslavement to magazine writing. Unfortunately, it also marks the beginning of his final decline. While he was living in Hollywood without Mia, Agee sloughed off what little restraint he had previously exercised. Overwork, drinking, and smoking increased. His sexual liaisons tested even Mia's tolerance. Though he was intensely aware that he was growing older, Agee behaved as though he were a much younger man, with typical lack of control with regard to his health. On January 15, 1951, he suffered his first major heart attack. Though he was, as always, concerned with the effect of his actions on others, Agee was unable or unwilling to take the necessary precautions to protect his own health.[17] Even reunion with Mia, who had been a positive influence, did not lead to more healthful habits. In 1955, at the age of forty-five, just two days short of the anniversary of his father's death, James Agee died of a heart attack. He left behind an intense and poetic autobiographical novel; an unclassifiable, virtually indescribable book about tenant farmers and about the man who lived among them; a shorter novel and a number of short stories, poems, and screenplays; many articles and reviews written for *Fortune, Time,* and other magazines; sad, salty, passionate letters and journal entries; and the lingering sense that, given the discipline, the money, the restraint, or the life he might have lived, he would have left behind a great deal more.

## Notes

1. See, e.g., the "darkness" passage in Agee, *A Death in the Family* (New York: McDowell, Obolensky, 1957), 80–96.
2. For several examples of Agee's references to his problem with depression, see *Letters of James Agee to Father Flye* (New York: Braziller, 1962), 40, 42, 56–57, 84–85, 170, 185, 194–95.
3. Kenneth Seib, *James Agee: Promise and Fulfillment* (Pittsburgh: U of Pittsburgh P, 1968), 3.
4. Mark A. Doty, *Tell Me Who I Am: James Agee's Search for Selfhood* (Baton Rouge: Louisiana State UP, 1981), 7.
5. Father James H. Flye, "An Article of Faith," in *Remembering James Agee*, ed. David Madden (Baton Rouge: Louisiana State UP, 1974), 17.
6. *Letters of James Agee to Father Flye,* 46–47.
7. Laurence Bergreen, *James Agee: A Life* (New York: Dutton, 1984), 107–9.
8. *Letters of James Agee to Father Flye,* 72.
9. Seib, *James Agee: Promise and Fulfillment,* 8–9, 12–13. See also Geneviève Moreau, *The Restless Journey of James Agee,* trans. Miriam Kleiger and Morty Schiff (New York: Morrow, 1977), 17, 183, 206–7, 255; Dwight Macdonald, "Jim Agee, A Memoir," in *Remembering James Agee,* ed. Madden, 134, 137–38; and *Letters of James Agee to Father Flye,* 137.

10. Doty, *Tell Me Who I Am*, 58; *Letters of James Agee to Father Flye*, 51–52.
11. Doty, *Tell Me Who I Am*, 59.
12. Bergreen, *James Agee: A Life*, 210–11, 225.
13. John Hersey, "Introduction: Agee," in *Three Tenant Families: Let Us Now Praise Famous Men*, by James Agee and Walker Evans (Boston: Houghton, 1988), xxiv, xxv.
14. Bergreen, *James Agee: A Life*, 250.
15. Mia Agee with Gerald Locklin, "Faint Lines in a Drawing of Jim," in *Remembering James Agee*, ed. Madden, 159.
16. Doty, *Tell Me Who I Am*, 68.
17. Doty, *Tell Me Who I Am*, 56, 124. See also Macdonald, "Jim Agee, A Memoir," 142; Robert Fitzgerald, "A Memoir," in *Remembering James Agee*, ed. Madden, 52; and *Letters of James Agee to Father Flye*, 125–27, 198, 188–89, 202–3, 212, 210.

# The Lost World of Agee's
## *Let Us Now Praise Famous Men*

### *George Brown Tindall*

MY FUNCTION IN THIS ESSAY is something like that of stage technician—to install the set for the performance that is to follow, to supply the backdrop for other scholars who seek to interpret selected aspects of James Agee's first major work in prose. Perhaps I should explain at the outset, too, that this particular piece will have less to do with James Agee and Walker Evans themselves, or their work, than it has to do with the world of their masterpiece, *Let Us Now Praise Famous Men.*

The title, a quotation from the apocryphal book of *Ecclesiasticus,* was of course used ironically. The book told about people who were anything but famous—until Agee made them so. My subject will be the lost world of tenancy and sharecropping—how it came to be and how it has vanished in the years since Agee visited Alabama—in large part fairly soon after he left Alabama.

Professor E. C. Branson, a rural sociologist who had pioneered the study of sociology at the University of North Carolina, wrote in the early 1920s that southern tenancy had drifted into "villeinage that begins to approach the sixteenth-century type."[1] Branson's colleague S. H. Hobbs a few years later wrote: "The greatest single economic and social problem . . . throughout the South is farm tenancy."[2] The finest piece of scholarship on the old one-crop cotton-culture complex of the South was Rupert B. Vance's *Human Factors in Cotton Cul-*

*ture*.[3] The book originated in Chapel Hill as a dissertation, written by a sociologist who was also a closet historian and who wielded the English language with a grace and clarity not always imputed to either trade.

Yet little of these studies penetrated very far into public awareness. Any real attention to the problem, a discerning journalist of the 1920s wrote, would require " a Charles Dickens whose genius might put the tenant farmer so starkly before Mr. Babbitt's imagination that he would be galvanized into a fury of activity."[4] Several such novelists appeared in the 1920s. The best was Kentuckian Elizabeth Madox Roberts, whose book, *The Time of Man* (1926), got far less attention than it deserved. It told the story of young Ellen Chesser, a tenant girl who dreamed of a home of her own. Ellen gradually moved from youthful exuberance through adolescent disillusionment to adult resignation as the wife of a migratory tenant, but aboard a wagon piled with their pitiful possessions she could still nourish the faint hope of "Some better country. Our own place maybe. Our trees in the orchard. Our own land sometime. Our own place to keep."[5] But her story ended with the dream of some better country always beyond reach. She never found her own place, and if she had, she no doubt would have found it a disappointment.

Agee's visit with the Alabama tenants came just ten years after *The Time of Man* and his book five years after that. It captured a fashion of working people as victims and objects of reform, as protagonists and heroes during the depression years, a vogue that flourished in the worlds of journalism and literature, of entertainment and scholarship, of art and politics. The book fit more specifically a subcategory of the rural poor, tenants and sharecroppers, a fashion inspired especially by the popularity of Erskine Caldwell's *Tobacco Road* (1932).

The vogue ran through such works as Herbert Harrison Kroll's *Cabin in the Cotton* (1931) and *I Was a Sharecropper* (1937), Charlie May Simon's *The Share-Cropper* (1937), and many another book now forgotten. The masterpiece of the "proletarian" novels on rural displacement was John Steinbeck's *The Grapes of Wrath* (1939), which pictured the wanderings of the uprooted "Okies" and "Arkies" in the odyssey of the Joad family, drawn by the illusory promise of jobs in a California already overloaded with farm labor. Those who managed to stay, and their descendants, have turned much of California's Central and Imperial valleys into a kind of western colony of the South, where grits and southern accents abound.[6]

Three of the titles just mentioned come readily to mind because they were turned into motion-picture hits. *Tobacco Road* was also a hit on the Broadway stage, more for the scandal it evoked than for its message. The subject matter is hardly funny, yet poking fun at poor whites is an old tradition of southern humor, and the southern redneck is the last ethnic group left that is fair game in the media today. The film of Kroll's *Cabin in the Cotton* included one of the funniest lines ever uttered in a movie. In the plantation store the landlord's daughter sidled up to the leader of protesting tenants, whom she had been tantalizing all along, and said: "I'd love to kiss you, but I just washed my hair." Bette Davis has said that the line, written into the scenario by playwright Paul Green, is her favorite of any she ever spoke before the camera.[7] *The Grapes of Wrath* includes what to me is one of the most moving episodes in these films. The Joad family, after many tribulations, finally checked into a migrant labor camp run by "the government," surely the New Deal's Farm Security Administration. The young Tom Joad, played by Henry Fonda, turned back after checking in to thank the manager for his courtesy to Tom's mother. "Ma's sure gonna like it here," he said. "She ain't been treated decent for a long while." Tenants and sharecroppers, Agee wrote, were "an undefended and appallingly damaged group of human beings."[8] Fear, ingrained by experience, was their constant lot, by the testimony of one observer after another.

These films were of course fictional, but they conveyed truth to millions of viewers who never saw the studies of tenancy and sharecropping that scholars had ground out since before the turn of the century. Even the scholarship on tenancy got more attention as the New Deal focused on social problems and the tenant farmers themselves found voice in the Southern Tenant Farmers Union, founded in 1934. One of the most intensive studies was Arthur Raper's *Preface to Peasantry* (1934), a comparison of two Georgia black-belt counties, along with other studies such as Charles S. Johnson's *Shadow of the Plantation* (1934) and Margaret Jarman Hagood's *Mothers of the South: Portraiture of the White Tenant Farm Woman* (1939). But the most influential study was a thin, concentrated description of the problem, *The Collapse of Cotton Tenancy* (1935), compiled by three men: Charles S. Johnson, Edwin Embree, and Will Alexander. Based on statistical and field surveys by Johnson's students at Fisk University and by Rupert Vance at the University of North Carolina at Chapel Hill, it recommended a federal program to deal with tenancy. It was promoted by a skilled press agent who put it on front pages across the country and contrived to get a copy on President Roosevelt's desk.[9]

*Let Us Now Praise Famous Men* in many parts and many ways dealt less with tenants than with Agee himself, a middle-class young man, a graduate of elite schools, turned into a kind of Old Testament prophet, a latter-day Amos or Micah, filled with pity and anger at the oppression of the poor whom he had seen mostly from afar before he went briefly to live with them. His book, of course, was sui generis, but in contemporary terms it belonged to the documentation, social exploration, and descriptive journalism that formed what critic Alfred Kazin called the "now innocent, now calculating, now purely rhetorical, but always significant experience in national self-discovery" that occurred in the 1930s.[10] This experience also found expression in such books as *These Are Our Lives*, in which the Federal Writers' Project gathered case histories of workers and sharecroppers in Georgia, North Carolina, and Tennessee, a pioneering work in the oral history of the "inarticulate."[11]

Agee's book belongs in a subcategory of treatments combining social reportage with photographic illustration such as: Erskine Caldwell and Margaret Bourke-White, *You Have Seen Their Faces* (1937), and *Say, Is This the USA?* (1941); Dorothea Lange and Paul S. Taylor, *An American Exodus* (1939). Under the direction of Roy Stryker the Farm Security Administration built up a unique photographic documentation of the life of the people.[12] Among the ways in which the Agee-Evans collaboration is unique are its focus and the fact that, while it originated as a 1936 project for an article in *Fortune* magazine, it did not appear as a book until August 1941, just four months before Pearl Harbor. It sold only six hundred copies before Agee died in 1955. Yet after re-publication in 1960 it came to be hailed as a classic of journalism and literature. It is better known now than studies that influenced New Deal policies, its recognition delayed ironically by the public focus on World War II, which did more than New Deal policy to shatter the old system of farm tenure.

But this is to get ahead of the story. What of the system in which the three families of the book were mired? How did it start? "How did we get caught? Why is it things always seem to go against us?" Agee asked in what appears to be his own meditation on the thoughts of his subjects. "What, what is it has happened? What is it has been happening that we are living the way we are?"[13] Years later a reporter found Ruby Fields Darley ("Pearl Woods" in the book), who recalled her brother's fury at Walker Evans's picture, which "looked like it was back in slavery time." She paused and said, "Well, I guess in a way it was."[14]

Indeed, tenancy was rooted in the tragedy of slavery and its aftermath. Even dedicated abolitionists, save a few of the most radical, shrank from measures of land reform that might have given freedmen a measure of self-support and independence. Citizenship and legal rights were one thing, wholesale land distribution another. Instead, with a few notable exceptions on confiscated lands, the slaves were turned loose without homes and without means of support other than their own labor.

Many optimists thought they saw a breakup of the plantation. In 1880 the poet Sidney Lanier brought forth one of those perennial essays on "The New South," which we still see a century later. "The New South means small farming," he wrote. "The quiet rise of the small farmer" was "the notable circumstance of the period, in comparison with which noisier events signify nothing."[15] But the growth of small farming was a statistical illusion. Farms of all sizes were more numerous because new acreage was coming into cultivation, even in the old seaboard states. The census, moreover, counted tenant and sharecropper plots as separate farms.

Small farming, in fact, had been more common in the Old South than it came to be later. Far more white southerners lived on yeoman subsistence farms than on plantations, but in the postwar era they were drawn more and more into the market economy. King Cotton survived the war and extended his sway over new acreage and new subjects as he expanded westward. But the growing European markets (mainly English) that had supported the commitment to cotton leveled off after the Civil War while the cotton belt continued to grow and prices declined.[16]

Sharecropping and tenancy developed as a compromise between the landlords' preference for supervised gang labor and the freedmen's hopes of independence and property. The inefficiencies of the system became more and more prevalent in the aftermath of emancipation, but seldom did the system produce the self-sufficiency that Lanier envisioned. Generally the reality fell somewhere between the freedmen's hopes of independence (forty acres and a mule) and the landlords' wish for a supervised work force.[17] The sharecropper, who had nothing to offer but his labor, tilled the land in return for supplies and a share of the crop, generally about half. The tenant farmer, only imperceptibly better off, might offer a mule, a plow, perhaps an independent line of credit at the country store, and therefore might claim a larger share, commonly three-fourths of the cash crop and two-thirds of the subsistence crop, which was mainly corn. There were, moreover, infinite variations plus other arrangements ranging from cash rental to outright peonage. From the standpoint of efficiency, the dominant system approached the worst conceivable arrangement, for the tenant lacked incentive to care for the land and the owner had little chance to supervise the work. These systems, moreover, bred a morbid suspicion on both sides. The folklore of the South was replete with stories of tenants who remained stubbornly shiftless and improvident. And, in fact, experience taught that prudent investment in a mule or plow might go to settle accounts the next bad year. Far better to spend a windfall on transient pleasure. On the other side one found stories of landlords who kept books with crooked pencils, as they had ample chance to do.

The crop-lien system was equally flawed. The most that could be said for it was that it supplied credit in a situation where cash was scarce. Country merchants furnished supplies in return for a lien (or mortgage) on the crop. To a few tenants and small farmers who seized the opportunity the credit afforded independence, but to most it afforded only the hopeless rounds of perennial debt. The merchant assumed great risks but more often than not had a territorial monopoly—distances and bad roads kept farmers from competitors—and the merchant deliberately exploited his power to lock in farmers to the cash crop at the expense of subsistence, which the merchant supplied at the cost of markups and interest rates which remained, more often than not, a mystery to the purchaser.[18] For all the wind and ink expended on preachments of diversification, the routines of tenancy and sharecropping yielded only with difficulty to other arrangements: the marketing, supply, and credit systems were geared to the staple crop, usually cotton.

For generations the rural South sank into the morass. In 1880 tenants worked 36.2 percent of all southern farms; by 1920, 49.6 percent; in 1930, 55.5 percent. Increasingly the typical tenant was white, two out of three in 1935, the year before Agee and Evans reached Alabama. Of all white farm operators nearly half were tenants; of blacks more than two-thirds. In all, tenant families included perhaps 5.5 million whites and more than 3 million blacks, about one of every four southerners.[19]

When Agee and Evans visited Alabama, they little realized that they were witness to the last generation of southern sharecroppers, that their personal observations came just as the system reached its peak and began to decline. By the time the book appeared in 1941 the decline of sharecropping had already set in—as of sometime in the mid-1930s. From Eli Whitney's invention of the cotton gin in 1793 to the end of the Civil War in 1865—the heyday of the slave system—seventy-two years elapsed, just over the Biblical three score and ten. From then until the date of the Agee-Evans visit to Alabama is a span of seventy-one years, during which tenancy and sharecropping flourished

The flawed economy of the postbellum South was a legacy of slavery and racial prejudice, a system that stymied innovation and development. By the turn of the century the stagnation of rural life had drawn more white people than black into bondage to privation and ignorance. In the short run it may have been the best of all possible worlds, given the tragic legacy of the past—or maybe the only possible world—but in the long run it became a stagnant world in which the routines of sharecropping and tenancy, the crop lien and the commodity markets, yielded slowly to other possibilities, and ultimately only to the shock of outside forces. Between 1890 and 1921 the boll weevil enveloped the whole cotton belt; black and white southerners formed an exodus toward a national labor market. Ultimately, however, the system gave way only to the Great Depression, the New Deal, World War II, and mechanization.

The New Deal was already hastening the disappearance of the system by its farm program, which reduced production to raise prices. Harvested acreage in cotton went down from 44,768,000 in 1929 to 22,800,000 in 1939.[20] Benefit payments to farmers were supposed to go in part to tenants, but only a trickle found its way to them. They were grateful nonetheless for meager rehabilitation programs as well as, after 1937, the Farm Tenant Act administered by the Farm Security Administration, a short-lived effort to help tenants buy their own farms.

The transformation of the cotton culture—in fact its departure from large parts of the Southeast—was already far advanced by the end of the 1930s. World War II further undermined the system by taking people off the farm into military service and into shipyards, factories, and other jobs in which they learned new skills and broadened their horizons. Briefly, at the end of the war, there was a return to the land, but it lasted only about a year before the exodus renewed. The rapid advance in mechanization of the farms after the war was probably less a force in driving labor from the land than it was a response to labor's flight from the land. By 1950 most southerners were in citified jobs in manufacturing or in trade, service, and professional occupations.

All along there had been forces contributing to a southern "enclosure movement." For those familiar with European history, the term *enclosure* summons up old scenes of peasants set adrift by landlords' engrossment of rural lands to produce wool or whatever. The South's turn arrived in the twentieth century. In his *Breaking the Land,* historian Pete Daniel several years ago said: "The process of dispossession began with the eviction of sharecroppers, and it continues with the failure of millionaire farmers."[21] The tendencies toward enclosure, already visible a century ago, were nurtured by governmental intrusion and by mechanization, which made traditional farm cultures conform more to visions of efficiency born in the nineteenth-century agricultural colleges and experiment stations and nurtured in the twentieth century. A central agency in the transformation was the Extension Service, created by Congress in 1914, and its army of county demonstration agents. As agriculture has become more and more businesslike, it has become, like most businesses, more capital intensive than labor intensive. And the factories in the fields, like the factories in the towns, rely on wage labor.

Within the last decade historians, journalists, and filmmakers have sought out the survivors among those who appeared in Walker Evans's pictures and their descendants. None of the three families— whom Agee called Ricketts, Woods, and Gudger in the book, and who were respectively Tingle, Fields, and Burroughs in real life—has lived a rags-to-riches story. They have followed millions of other southerners in the exodus from sharecropping and tenancy, but few have joined the exodus to far places. Most remain in or near Hale County, Alabama.[22] One of the Burroughs boys appeared in the documentary film, "Let Us Now Praise Famous Men Revisited" He is the only one still employed in agriculture—but as a wage laborer. Working with tractors and mechanical cotton pickers, he said he could do in one day what just twenty years ago it took forty people to do.

Over two or three generations these families have worked in factories, rest homes, and various other occupations and have moved up in large part from the tenant shacks to the mobile home. One of the original elders, Frank Tingle ("Fred Ricketts" in the book) actually achieved that impossible dream of every tenant, to become a farm owner himself. Head of a family clearly the least regarded in the community, he was the only one to secure a government loan under the New Deal's Farm Tenant Act. In 1929 he got 129 acres, and when a storm swept the land, he made enough off the timber it felled to pay off the loan. He lived to the ripe age of ninety, and the place passed on to his daughter Elizabeth. The farm, however, according to those who have visited it, exists in a time warp, a degraded remnant of the sharecropper world of poverty, a bitter testimonial to the Southern Tenant Farmers Union's prediction that the small farm would be a formula for poverty.

The future lay with the large farm which could best exploit science and technology. The only choice would be between the large-scale cooperative farm on the one hand and the large landholder or corporation on the other. We all know what the choice was. It had, in fact, already been made when the Tenant Farmers Union spoke in 1937.

And the evidence found by the most recent visitors to the land cultivated by the Rickettses, Woodses, and Gudgers suggests that the end of tenancy left most of their descendents about where an English visitor found the collapse of slavery had left the earlier generation: "The human wreckage left by the collapse had been allowed to drift aimlessly about for sixty years."[23]

## Notes

1.    E. C. Branson, "Farm Tenancy in the Cotton Belt: How Farm Tenants Live," *Journal of Social Forces* 1 (Mar. 1923): 213.

2.    Samuel H. Hobbs, Jr., *North Carolina: Economic and Social* (Chapel Hill: U of North Carolina P, 1930), 451.

3.    Rupert B. Vance, *Human Factors in Cotton Culture* (Chapel Hill: U of North Carolina P, 1929).

4.    Gerald W. Johnson, "Mr. Babbitt Arrives at Erzerum," *Journal of Social Forces* 1 (Mar. 1923): 208.

5.    Elizabeth Madox Roberts, *The Time of Man, A Novel* (New York: Viking, 1926), 382.

6.    James Noble Gregory, *American Exodus: The Dust Bowl Migration and Okie Culture in California* (New York: Oxford UP, 1989).

7.    Whitney Stine, with running commentary by Bette Davis, *Mother Goddam: The Story of the Career of Bette Davis* (New York: Hawthorne, 1974), 36–37.

8.    James Agee and Walker Evans, *Let Us Now Praise Famous Men* (Boston: Houghton, 1941), 7.

9.    George Brown Tindall, *The Emergence of the New South* (Baton Rouge: Louisiana State UP, 1967), 416.

10.    Alfred Kazin, *On Native Grounds: An Interpretation of Modern American Prose Literature* (New York: Reynal & Hitchcock, 1942), 485.

11.    Federal Writers' Project, *These Are Our Lives* (Chapel Hill: U of North Carolina P, 1939).

12.    F. Jack Hurley, *Portrait of a Decade: Roy Stryker and the Development of Documentary Photography in the Thirties* (Baton Rouge: Louisiana State UP, 1972).

13.    Agee and Evans, *Let Us Now Praise Famous Men*, 80, 81.

14.    Howell Raines, "Let Us Now Revisit Famous Folk," *New York Times Magazine*, 25 May 1980, 32.

15.    Sidney Lanier, "The New South," *Scribner's Monthly* 20 (Oct. 1880): 840.

16.    Gavin Wright, *The Political Economy of the Cotton South: Households, Markets, and Wealth in the Nineteenth Century* (New York: Norton, 1978), 158–84.

17.    Roger Ransom and Richard Sutch, *One Kind of Freedom: The Economic Consequences of Emancipation* (New York: Cambridge UP, 1977), 56–103.

apathetic, and depressed from ennui, despair, guilt, shame, "gallop-ing melancholia," self-doubt, cold fear, self-pity, self-hatred, remorse, in-ability to atone, insomnia, work-blockage. But he also expressed ecstasy and enthusiasm and many other positive moods of rare quality. He emerges above all, boy and man, as painfully scrupulous.

One of the most intellectual and analytical of modern American writers, Agee denied on every occasion that he was intellectualizing; he advocated constantly, in abstract terms, the necessity to rely mainly on instinct, the senses. He was hypnotized by his own rhetoric in some passages of almost everything he wrote. His proclaimed antipa-thy to art was always expressed in the most artistic context, concepts, and diction. Even as he jeeringly cautions his readers not to call *Fa-mous Men* a work of art, every page bears witness to his struggle to achieve nothing less. And a few pages after he laments his lack of imagination, he expresses a resentment of the "deifying of the imagi-nation."[3]

Agee struggled with conflicting attitudes about religion (Protes-tantism, Episcopalianism, Catholicism), politics (communism, anar-chism), and art (adoration, revulsion). He had enormous veneration for life but was often suicidal. He wanted family life but was drawn to bohemianism. He who explored so many possibilities in art forms saw his life as a series of lost opportunities. His own vocation, as he said of Gauguin's, was "like a lure set out by God"; he would find after many years that "it was not the real thing even but only the lure and that all it was trying to teach him was to be as absolutely faithful to his own soul and his own being as he could, and that he find out the price of that as he went along."[4]

Few writers have been as obsessed as Agee was with analyzing the difficulties of the creative process, and in the work of few writers has the process been so much the subject of the work itself. No writer was ever as self-revealing, self-doubting, guilt-ridden as Agee is in *Fa-mous Men*. His obsession with original sin and the moral sin of pride helps to explain his avocation of failure. Agee felt unworthy facing the task, sinful in the act of performing it, guilty for the finished work:

> To come devotedly into the depths of a subject, your respect for it
> increasing in every step and your whole heart weakening apart with

shame upon yourself in your dealing with it: To know at length better and better and at length into the bottom of your soul your unworthiness of it: Let me hope in any case that it is something to have begun to learn. (319)

The subtle dialectics of sin and guilt pervade his life and work. The very things before which he shivered in awe, in fear, or ecstasy, Agee felt he eventually betrayed. Somewhere in the tension between self-destructive guilt and creative overreaching, Agee expressed his finest moments of emotional and mental consciousness. He seemed to need some form of punishment simultaneous with joy, as when he lay on George Gudger's mattress, vermin biting his flesh, his spirit perfectly attuned to the spirits of the inhabitants.

Few other modern writers have been as conscious of the reader as Agee is in *Famous Men*. For him, the reader needed not only to be scolded and abused and occasionally reviled but also to be exhorted to collaborate with the author in a brotherhood of imagination. Through repeated direct address, Agee draws his reader into the conscious process of creation, for this "is a human effort which must require human co-operation" (111). The problems some readers have with *Famous Men* mirror Agee's own in writing it. The act of writing a book is often an unwritten drama that parallels the story being written. In unique ways, Agee works that drama into the book itself; it became two books, progressing in counterpoint. Agee repeatedly talks of the limits of prose and of his own inability to express what he feels a compulsion to tell us. The reader goes through various stages in his lifelong communion with this book: resistance, reluctant surrender, total surrender, afterthoughts, withdrawal, return.

When one first reads *Famous Men*, many passages may strike one as pretentious, mannered, precious, pompous, pontifical, smug, self-righteous, self-indulgent, willfully obscure, doctrinaire, self-congratulatory, sophomoric, belligerent; even Agee's self-abnegation, self-loathing, and modesty may offend. One may eventually come to regard these faults as inseparable from the book's virtues.

One objection is that Agee's style is far too prolix, too derivative, a pastiche of great writers—Shakespeare, Gerard Manley Hopkins, Henry James, Thomas Wolfe, William Faulkner; that it is too arty, too literary, full of Elizabethan, Biblical inverted phrasing and cadence, with a Harvard accent; that it is as self-consciously odd in punctuation and typography as e. e. cummings; that it is sometimes more abstract than philosophy is, as in "Colon," and sometimes more specific than journalism is, as in "Work 2: Cotton." Agee does not heed Ezra Pound's admonition to the Imagist poets: "Go in fear of abstractions."[5] For readers who would rather have it plain, Agee, when he is simple, is very effective indeed.

Too much of the book, some complain, is about Agee's own reactions to the life of the tenant families, too little about the people themselves. Some complain that his romanticization of their poverty is offensive, a little like romanticizing the Holocaust. In his sentimental approach, Agee may seem "more concerned with God's creatures than God is."[6] His notebooks are more sentimental than the finished book, suggesting he consciously dealt with the problem. Camus, in the first entry in his *Notebooks*, May 1935, says, "One can, with no romanticism, feel nostalgic for lost poverty."[7] Agee was indeed afflicted with a terrible nostalgia—for a lost rural childhood he never really had.

Agee asks his readers to forget that this is a book; many can't. He anticipates the charge that it is a "mess." What, then, is it? What does it deal with, what does it not deal with? Some say Agee couldn't decide whether he was writing a documentary or an autobiography, a journal, philosophy, sociology, history, aesthetics, a treatise on education, politics, music, art, or photography. In some libraries it is cataloged under agriculture (Agee might have liked that). The book deals with all these subjects, cutting across categories.

Some readers call *Let Us Now Praise Famous Men* the *Moby-Dick* of nonfiction. Melville's autobiographical narrator, Ishmael, tells about Ahab and other men living and working under the special circumstances of whale hunting. That novel too could have been called *Let Us Now Praise Famous Men.* Ishmael's first-person narration is only a device; we soon forget him (he is seldom more than a witness), and it is Melville's own searching voice we follow. The "Cetology" and the "Whiteness of the Whale" chapters exhibit the kind of polarity that is characteristic of both books. Like Agee, Melville often talks to the reader about the mechanics and difficulties of writing the book; the whale Melville pursues is the book itself.

Other readers see qualities of *Walden* in Agee's book. Speaking directly in his own lyrical voice, Thoreau focuses not upon men in nature but upon the external world in ways that enable him to reveal the internal world. He could have called his book *Thoreau*. It, too, exhibits—in "Economy" and "Solitude," for instance—the kind of polarities between which Agee struggled. The extrovert Melville of *Moby-Dick* and the introvert Thoreau of *Walden* are combined in the Agee of *Let Us Now Praise Famous Men*.

The transformation of historical, political, and social factual material by the lyric impulse is unusual among those southern writers of Agee's time who took on the task of dealing with such material. Consider writers born or living and writing in Tennessee. In the late twenties and early thirties, three Agrarians wrote biographies of Civil War figures: Allen Tate's *Stonewall Jackson, the Good Soldier* (1928) and *Jefferson Davis, His Rise and Fall* (1929); Robert Penn Warren's *John Brown, the Making of a Martyr* (1929); and Andrew Lytle's *Bedford Forrest and His Critter Company* (1931). Neither in those books nor even in the book in which they stated their relation to their varied southern material, *I'll Take My Stand* (1930), did they express the kind of agony of conscience and spirit and the artistic qualms that are part of the achievement and failure of *Famous Men*. In dealing with historical material, they all maintained an attitude of ironic and philosophical distance.

Evelyn Scott, a Clarksville, Tennessee, novelist and poet who was never associated with the Fugitives or the Agrarians, approached, on the other hand, the writing of *Background in Tennessee* (1937) with the realization that "all I possessed which might be regarded as Tennessee documenta to be presented to a public, seemed to be myself. . . ."[8] In "The Woman in the Foreground," Peggy Bach, Scott's biographer, wrote: "Always intruding upon the formal history of Tennessee are Scott's poignant memories."[9] Compared with Agee's book, Scott's is clearly autobiography and history intertwined, making use of techniques and a style similar to her experimental memoir, *Escapade*, set in rural Brazil during six years of poverty and illness. One wonders whether Agee read it.

Before and soon after the publication of *Famous Men*, two fictional characters appeared who resemble Agee in their struggle with factual material: Faulkner's Quentin Compson and Warren's Jack

Burden, both of whom may be said to be undergoing Fitzgerald's "test of a first-rate intelligence." Quentin, Faulkner's most autobiographical character, suffers division in every aspect of his life. In "That Evening Sun" (1931) and in several other short stories, he is unconscious of the division; in his section of *The Sound and the Fury* (1929), he is so unconscious of the division that he commits suicide; in *Absalom, Absalom!* he sublimates the dynamics of that division of self. In the appendix to *Famous Men*, Agee cites Thomas Wolfe and Faulkner. If Agee's life exhibited the gusto of Wolfe's, his writing was excruciatingly meditative, like Quentin's.

In *All the King's Men* (1946), Jack Burden is, like Agee and Quentin, divided in his attitudes toward his two great writing goals: his doctoral dissertation in history about his kinsman Cass Mastern in the historical setting of the Civil War and his journalistic report on Willie Stark in the Great Depression. Both stories become, for the reader, Jack Burden's autobiography. All first-person narratives, whether fiction or nonfiction, whether ostensibly about another person or about oneself, express facets of the narrator's own life, especially those written out of the agony of conscious or unconscious divided purpose. The working out of that agony—usually without resolution—is the process that is rendered.

Superficially, *Famous Men* is like the many other books on the Great Depression published throughout the thirties: the photo-text books, the proletarian novels, the eyewitness commentaries, the protest plays, the social-consciousness art and photography. While a number of southern and northern poets and fiction writers combined their words with the photographs of others during the 1930s, only Wright Morris juxtaposed his own photographs with his own words to create two experimental books that by comparison and contrast may help us to see the Agee-Evans achievement more clearly. In the 1940 *New Directions in Prose and Poetry* annual, James Laughlin paired photo-text selections from Morris's still-evolving book *The Inhabitants* with selections from the soon-to-be-published *Let Us Now Praise Famous Men*, under the heading "The American Scene." (The year is given erroneously as 1936 in Agee bibliographies.) He hailed Morris's work as a major achievement and placed its 27 pages before the 14 devoted to the work of Agee and Evans. Morris's introductory note deals with the relation of technique to substance, of words to photographs, though without the agony of Agee's passages on the same themes in the book itself. Although his photographs, usually without people, resemble those by Evans that contain no human images, Morris was shooting as early as 1935. Still, he felt certain affinities for Agee and Evans, often commenting on *Famous Men*, especially in "Privacy as a Subject for Photography" (1951), *About Fiction* (1975), and *Earthly Delights, Unearthly Adornments* (1978). Short lyrical prose pieces appear opposite photographs in *The Inhabitants* (not published until 1946); *The Home Place* (1948) is a lyrical first-person novel, with a photograph on every other of its 176 pages. The relationship between photographs and prose is, in both books, not literal but symbiotic. Morris told me in 1989 that he has always felt such empathy for Agee (whom he met once, briefly) that while he was writing *The Deep Sleep* he did not read Agee, afraid he might be influenced. There are so many affinities between *The Deep Sleep* (1953) and *A Death in the Family*, which appeared four years after Morris's novel, that one is tempted to wonder whether Agee might have been influenced by Morris.

Father Flye and others have called *Famous Men* a religious book, a spiritual odyssey or quest. It is full of religious terminology, and the religious ambience of the book does tend to create a unity of effect. A mystical note reverberates throughout Agee's work and the work of those who write about him. In Alabama, everything was runic to Agee, iconic; talismanic objects seemed inhabited by the spirits of those who had used them. With the mobility of the movie-camera eye, which had awed him early in his life, Agee's omniscient vision moved among the tenant families. "What could be more moving, significant or true: every force and hidden chance in the universe has so combined that a certain thing was the way it was" (241). His lifelong compulsion was to see mirrors face to face, endlessly reflecting each other, himself and others, himself and the tenant families. He strove to achieve an intuitive simultaneity of all things, a perfect communion. In exerting all his consciousness in an "effort to perceive simply the cruel radiance of what is" (11) Agee tried, says Robert Coles, to render "an actuality that only God can."[10] In Alabama, he was God's spy. *Famous Men* aspires, in its pride, to be scripture-like, a quality Wright Morris attributes to it.

Its eccentricities of form give many readers difficulty as they struggle to master the pattern or structure of the book. Agee's comments in the book itself describe his own attitude and task. But in his application for a Guggenheim fellowship, he gave some helpful preliminary explanations. The approach will be "anti-artistic, anti-scientific, and anti-journalistic," though analytic, in method and attitude. Traditional forms will be used, but parts will have "many of the qualities of a novel, a report, poetry . . . new forms of writing and of observation." It will be "a skeptical study of the nature of reality and of the false nature and re-creation and of communication"; his purpose will be "to tell everything possible as accurately as possible: and to invent nothing." A crucial part will be a "strict comparison of the photographs and the prose as relative liars and as relative reproducers of the same matters" (a task not undertaken directly in the finished work).[11] About the sharecroppers, Agee undertook:

> . . . not much yet some, to say: to say, what is his house: for whom does he work: under what arrangements and in what results: what is this work: who is he and where from, that he is now here; what is it his life has been and has done to him: what of his wife and of their children, each, for all these each is a life, a full universe: what are their clothes: what food is theirs to eat: what is it which is in their senses and their minds: what is the living and manner of their day, of a season, of a year: what, inward and outward, is their manner of living; of their spending and usage of these few years' openness out of the black vast and senseless death. . . . (110–11)

Perhaps the many kinds of elements work most effectively if we see Agee as the hero of the book—the hero as a nervous, fitful, nocturnal meditator. Everything, all the major elements in Agee's life and work converge in those eight weeks he spent in Alabama when he was twenty-eight (only four years out of Harvard) and in the act of writing *Famous Men*. In George Gudger, he resurrects the spirit of his father who, returning to his ancestral home, thinks, "This was the real, old, deep country, now. Home country. . . ."[12] In longing for that rural connection, Agee makes, in *Famous Men*, his own spiritual journey to his father's kind of land and people. To connect with his father's spirit, the child Rufus rubs his finger in his father's ash tray.

"He looked at his finger for a moment and licked it; his tongue tasted of darkness."[13] To connect with the Gudger family, adult Agee touches and smells their clothes. And the religious ritual element in *Famous Men* is an unconscious tribute to his mother's Episcopalianism. The conflicts, the polarities of his life, are reconciled in his Alabama experience and in this book.

Is *Famous Men* a failure? Yes, if one insists that it be a book like the others of that time, a kind of book Agee clearly never attempted. No, if one looks at Agee's own statements of purpose and the extent to which he achieved them. In this passage, he expresses his attitude toward writers and readers who see the sharecroppers as copy for journalists:

> It seems to me curious, not to say obscene and thoroughly terrifying ... to pry intimately into the lives of an undefended and appallingly damaged group of human beings ... for the purpose of parading the nakedness, disadvantage and humiliation of these lives before another group of human beings, in the name of science, of "honest journalism" (whatever that paradox many mean) ... for money ... and that these people could be capable of meditating this prospect ... with a conscience better than clear, and in the virtual certitude of almost unanimous public approval. (7)

This passage also expresses the conflict between Agee's own journalistic assignment and the impact of the experience itself, and between journalism and what he actually wrote.

Agee had a compulsion to transcend both the journalistic assignment and his own artistic aspirations. "This is not a work of art or entertainment, nor will I assume the obligations of the artist or entertainer" (111). "If I could do it, I'd do no writing at all here. It would be photographs; the rest would be fragments of cloth, bits of cotton, lumps of earth, records of speech, pieces of wood and iron, phials of odors" (13). Agee discovered that facts express very little. "You want the facts?" he seemed to ask. "These are the facts. Now, what are you going to do with them? File them away?" One must refuse to allow the misery people experience to swamp everything else; something must transcend the misery. Agee's insights are forged in the crucible of the moment, and it was his conviction that the medium of their expression ought, appropriately, to suffer the same time-fate. Thus, he wanted *Famous Men* printed on newsprint, so it would crumble in fifty years to dust (at about 1992).

Too often, southern writers and photographers expose without causing a revelation (Morris's phrase); even shocks of recognition are muffled by overexposure to sensational details and images. Agee taught new attitudes about the southern artist's task in working out his relation to his raw materials. One may sense in the fiction and photographs of the sixties and seventies overtones of the legacy of Agee and Evans. The best southern artists do not describe the region; they conceptualize it in an image. But most have not yet come into the full light of Agee's vision of the artist and worked, in their own ways, in and out of, with and against, that light.

With subjective, poetic language, Agee groped painfully for a metaphysical concept about the Alabama tenant family, their landscape, their artifacts. He wanted to create "an image of the very essence of their lives" (319). In the still and the moving camera eye, Agee caught epiphanic, charged images.

What attracts artists to the South are the artifacts on the scene. Artifacts that embody a concept of the spirit of the place for some artists often strike the average southerner as one species or another of junk. There are few "scenes" as such in *Famous Men*; rather, icons, figures on an urn—chairs, fireplaces, tables, stoves, dresses, shoes, overalls—take shape: ". . . a new suit of overalls has among its beauties those of a blueprint: and they are a map of a working man" (266). A house expresses the spirit of its inhabitants:

> . . . a house of simple people which stands empty and silent in the vast Southern country morning sunlight, and everything which on this morning in eternal space it by chance contains . . . shines forth with such grandeur, such sorrowful holiness . . . as no human consciousness shall ever rightly perceive, far less impart to another . . . there can be more beauty and more deep wonder in the standing and spacings of mute furnishings on a bare floor between the squaring bourns of walls than any music ever made. . . . (134)

> It is my belief that such houses as these . . . at times . . . achieve an extraordinary 'beauty.' In part because this is ordinarily neglected or

even misrepresented in favor of their shortcomings as shelters; and in part because their esthetic success seems to me even more important than their functional failure; and finally out of the uncontrollable effort to be faithful to my personal predilections, I have neglected function in favor of aesthetics. (202)

The "moral questions involved in evaluating" (202) such beauty vex him. He admits that he merely raises questions, "For I am in pain and uncertainty as to the answers." He feels that "one is qualified to insist on this [beauty] only in proportion as one faces the brunt of his own 'sin' in so doing." In a footnote, he says, "The 'sin,' in my present opinion, is in feeling in the least apologetic for perceiving the beauty of the houses." Agee asks, "Are things 'beautiful' which are not intended as such, but which are created in convergences of chance, need, innocence or ignorance, and for entirely irrelevant purposes" (203)? He concludes that "the partition wall of the Gudgers' front bedroom IS importantly among other things, a great tragic poem. . . . Upon the leisures of the earth the whole home is lifted before the approach of darkness as a boat and as a sacrament" (204).

What Agee could not do, time has done for him; it has brought into harmony the conflicting elements in *Famous Men.* The book and its readers are of the same general type today as they were in 1941—literary, socially concerned. The crucial difference is that the six hundred who bought the book in 1941 had been committed in the recent 1930s to ideals, and involved somehow in a struggle for justice, to which the factual material was relevant. The problem then was that the personal, lyrical material undercut the impact of the photographs and of the documentary material. But today, those elements are so familiar they have a museum-like, almost Smithsonian aura. Today, the book works mainly as lyric; the factual material is only one of several modes enhancing the lyrical.

"The volatile work," Agee says in *A Way of Seeing,* "is nearly always lyrical."[14] A metaphysical prose lyric, with mythic dimensions, *Famous Men* fulfills Ezra Pound's definition of great literature as "language charged with meaning [and emotion] to the utmost degree."[15] As for the outdated raw data presented in over half the book, another Pound pronouncement applies: "Literature is news that STAYS news."[16]

# Notes

A different version of this essay was published as a pamphlet to accompany the Special Classics Library edition of *Let Us Now Praise Famous Men* (Birmingham, AL: Oxmoor House, 1984).

1.  F. Scott Fitzgerald, *The Crack-Up* (New York: New Directions, 1945), 75.
2.  Ibid., 75.
3.  James Agee and Walker Evans, *Let Us Now Praise Famous Men* (Boston: Houghton, 1960), 241. All page references cited in the text are to this edition.
4.  James Agee, "Letter to a Friend," *James Agee: A Portrait* (New York: Caedmon Records TC 2042), side 2.
5.  Ezra Pound, "A Retrospect," in *Poets on Poetry*, ed. Charles Norman (New York: Free Press, 1965), 322.
6.  James Lee, on a panel discussing *Let Us Now Praise Famous Men* during Agee Week at St. Andrews School, Mounteagle, Tennessee, October 1972. For an account of that celebration, see the introduction to David Madden's *Remembering James Agee* (Baton Rouge: Louisiana State UP, 1974).
7.  Albert Camus, *Notebooks, 1935–1942*, ed. Philip Thody (New York: Knopf, 1963), 3.
8.  Evelyn Scott, *Background in Tennessee* (1937; rpt. Knoxville: U of Tennessee P, 1980), l.
9.  Peggy Bach, "The Woman in the Foreground," *Southern Review* 18 (Fall 1982): 711.
10. Robert Coles, "James Agee's 'Famous Men' Seen Again," *Harvard Advocate*, James Agee Commemorative Issue, 105.4 (Feb. 1972): 43.
11. James Agee, *Collected Short Prose of James Agee*, ed. Robert Fitzgerald (Boston: Houghton, 1969), 133–34.
12. James Agee, *A Death in the Family* (New York: McDowell, Obolensky, 1957), 48.
13. Ibid., 281.
14. James Agee, *A Way of Seeing: Photographs of New York by Helen Levitt* (New York: Viking Press, 1965), 5.
15. Ezra Pound, *A B C of Reading* (New York: New Directions, 1960), 28.
16. Ibid., 29.

# *Let Us Now Praise Famous Men*— and Women: Agee's Absorption in the Sexual

## *Linda Wagner-Martin*

JAMES AGEE'S *Let Us Now Praise Famous Men* has long been recognized as an amazingly innovative piece of writing. It draws upon a quantity of devices and themes from the high-modernist experimentation of William Faulkner, Thomas Wolfe, and John Dos Passos, and it offers an equal quantity of themes and devices toward the postmodernist experimentation to come: the self-reflexive interrogation of the narrator (Agee as author questioning Agee as character, and the reverse), the focused yet surreal visual effects, the Bakhtinian dialogic, and the pastiche of alternating objectivity and a subjectivity that ranges from maudlin to frightening. In Agee's own prose, he insists on the high seriousness of the work, claiming that if he were to do it right the reader "would hardly bear to live."[1] And when he explains how much of the actual he wants to force on the page, to make the gravest distillation of meaning possible, he writes,

> If I could do it, I'd do no writing at all here. It would be photographs; the rest would be fragments of cloth, bits of cotton, lumps of earth, records of speech, pieces of wood and iron, phials of odors, plates of food and of excrement. . . .
>
> A piece of the body torn out by the roots might be more to the point. (13)

In Agee's near-bombardment of virtuoso stylistic effects, one of his central and unifying strategies is surprisingly simple: it is the dominant role he gives to the characters of Annie Mae (Woods) Gudger, her sister Emma, her children, and her niece Ellen. So intense is Agee's formal attention to this group of female characters that *Let Us Now Praise Famous Men* becomes—at least in subtext—the romance of the wearily wasted Annie Mae or her surrogates and the well-placed voyeuristic narrator, James Agee. Because readers are asked to think of the portraits in the work as "real," and of Agee in his role of narrator/reporter as also "real," the high degree of fictionality of each has gone largely unremarked. In true post-modernist fashion, the reader must come to understand that the "character" of Annie Mae Gudger is no more real than the "character" of James Agee as narrator/reporter, as Agee has created him. Yet the narrative movement of the text derives much of its impetus from the character Agee's sexual fascination with the character of Annie Mae Gudger.

Agee makes Annie Mae and the related female characters central to the work through his choice and arrangement of narrative episodes and through the structure of the entire book. After lengthy preliminaries and apologies—in which Agee repeatedly refers to himself and Walker Evans as "spies," guilty interlopers in the world which, in pity and deference, might well ask that it be left alone—Agee opens the book proper (Book II) with the epigraph, "The house had now descended" (17). In the opening lines describing the bedroom of the sharecroppers' family, enclosing that family at sleep, Agee begins the haunting journey that ends where it begins, with the Gudger family at its most defenseless and intimate. In solemn, Whitmanic phrases, Agee introduces the family,

> In the square pine room at the back the bodies of the man of thirty and of his wife and of their children lay on shallow mattresses on their iron beds and on the rigid floor, and they were sleeping. (19)[2]

Agee establishes three important effects with this lengthy and varied beginning. (1) He presents the contradictory impression of Agee and Evans as spies, a description that floods the narrative with guilt and prompts the reader to question *why* this loving and wrenching portrayal produces guilt (suggesting the ambivalent reactions sex itself can invoke). (2) From the epigraph, the immediate presence of the house, made specific through the single modifier—*the*—brings the reader into the intimacy that such a referent suggests. There is only one house, and only one family, to absorb our interest, and in the passive and somewhat archaic verb—"had now descended"—one feels the structure settling around the reader as well as around the family. The process of enclosure may itself be both comforting and threatening, carrying out the ambivalence in the description. And (3) the description of the still family hints ominously that these are figures glimpsed in death, not sleep, as established by the opening phrase, "In the square pine room" ("square pine . . . box . . . coffin"). For all of Agee's seemingly objective detail, this is a highly ambivalent opening, its tones jostling rather than blending in the reader's mind.

The structure of the work repeats the uneasiness of its tone. The book appears in some ways to be like a house itself—forthright, forthcoming, with the more public and intellectualized matter given at the outside, arranged in layers around the seminal core of human life. In the outer layer, Agee adopts a Jamesian pose, musing on the role of the observer in fiction, on the kind of demands made by this difficult writing. In what he says *about* writing, however, he keeps the reader's attention on the three tenant families who are the subjects of his discourse; the distinctions he appears to establish are, finally, false. Inner penetrates outer; outer is but a threshold to the inner concerns. Rather than a boxlike structure, Agee's house of fiction becomes a vortex, a single center of focus.

False as well is Agee's emphasis, at key places in the narrative, on the externality one supposes from the sections entitled "On the Porch." Intensely homey, the vernacular "porch" creates a visual image as well as emphasizing the difference between public and private spheres (the reason Agee feels so guilty in this investigation). One assumes that a porch would be a public area, that admission to inner rooms would signal some greater receptiveness by the family members. Yet for these tenant families, much of their daily existence occurs on the porch, were air is cooler and conditions less crowded than inside the small house—and the physical freedom of the porch evokes some of the most meaningful language spoken by the family members. Agee's repetition of this "outside" location reinforces the distinction he attempts to draw between public and private, the distinction that actual circumstances reverse. Yet at this early point in the text, Agee's tactic of drawing the reader deep inside the house—whether the house of fiction or in actuality—is ironic because the narrator has *not* told the reader the most important things about the house: *whose it is, who* these sleepers are. In the introductory matter he has included a "cast of characters," the list of the three tenant families and what Agee calls "unpaid agitators"—William Blake, Sigmund Freud, Jesus Christ, others, again emphasizing the fabric of fiction and fact from which the text will grow. Even as the reader observes the sleeping family, then, that family has not been identified. Agee's trustworthiness as realistic narrator is accordingly called into question.

After this brief glimpse of the anonymous "sleepers," Agee moves abruptly to what he calls "the beginning," dating the next part of the book "July 1936." Evans and he are being driven to farmers' homes in search of fitting subjects for their study of sharecropping in the South during the Great Depression. Again, Agee stresses his betrayal of those subjects: he and Evans have asked that they be allowed to take some pictures, and one of their guides replies, "Sure, of course, take all the snaps you're a mind to." However, Agee reports, when the townspeople "saw the amount of equipment stowed in the back of our car, they showed that they felt they had been taken advantage of, but said nothing of it" (25). Poverty is silencing. What follows in *Let Us Now Praise Famous Men* is a series of three encounters, all with marginalized people who respond in the same voiceless way as the powerless farmers. Agee's and Evans's first encounter is with a black singing group, who speak in song rather than words, defiantly ready for any demand the white men may make. The second is with a trio of two ill or retarded men and a younger woman, described largely through her body's being "brass or bitter gold" (33). The third is with a young black couple, frightened at even having to deal with the strange white men. Here again, Agee uses the motion of the black woman's body to image her/their fear: "the young woman's whole body was jerked down tight as a fist into a crouch from which immediately, the rear foot skidding in the loose stone so that she nearly fell, like a kicked cow scrambling out of a creek, eyes crazy, chin stretched tight, she sprang forward into the first motions of a running not human but that of a suddenly terrified wild animal" (41). The reader's impression from the collage of scenes is that of fear, and the knowledge that poverty keeps people from language as much as does race or gender.

In the midst of this picaresque journey, Agee jumps in time—though perhaps not in tone—returning to the scene of the tenant family in its cramped bedroom. He explains carefully, "all in this house save myself are sleeping" (49) and then describes the bodies of the seven people in the room with all the passion he brings to his voyeuristic role. His sensual language emphasizes what he finds to be the illicit quality of his vision:

> Just a half-inch beyond the surface of this wall I face is another surface, one of the four walls which square and collaborate against the air another room, and there lie sleeping, on two iron beds and on pallets on the floor, a man and his wife and her sister, and four children, a girl and three harmed boys. (57)

Agee is soon to detail (dismember?) these separate bodies, defenseless before his scrutiny, private in their disarray and discomfort, but first he provides the reader with the tormented sense of what his involvement with this family means. His metaphor is blatantly sexual. "I know they rest and the profundity of their tiredness, as if I were in each one of these seven bodies whose sleeping I can almost touch through this wall, and which in the darkness I so clearly see, with the whole touch and weight of my body."

Agee, then, for the first time "introduces" the family members by name. The mystery of identity, however, rather than being solved, is deflected in the author's delineation of person as physical body. When George Gudger is described, for example, it is as "George's red body, already a little squat with the burden of thirty years, knotted like oakwood, in its clean white cotton summer union suit that it sleeps in." And the text continues, into what will become the vortex of the fiction,

> and his wife's beside him, Annie Mae's, slender, and sharpened through with bone, that ten years past must have had such beauty, and now is veined at the breast, and the skin of the breast translucent,

delicately shriveled, and blue, and she and her sister Emma are in
plain cotton shifts. (57)

Fusing the description of Annie Mae with that of her sister (who was
really George's sister, Mary) and following both with that of the oldest child, the daughter Louise, Agee assembles a montage of female
parts, ranging from mature to childlike, with no pause in the litany:
"and the body of Emma, her sister, strong, thick and wide, tall, the
breasts set wide and high, shallow and round, not yet those of a full
woman, the legs long thick and strong; and Louise's green lovely body,
the dim breasts faintly blown between wide shoulders, the thighs long,
clean and light in their line from hip to knee, the head back steep and
silent to the floor, the chin highest, and the white shift up to her divided thighs" (57–58).

Agee's narrative continues to emphasize the womanliness of whatever human interaction he chooses to show. A child awakes and Annie
Mae rouses to comfort him, speaking gently "in that cadence of strength
and sheltering comfort which anneals all fence of language and sur-
passes music" (58); the baby needs to be fed, from Annie Mae's breast;
it is increasingly clear that Annie Mae Gudger is the central symbol
for Agee's metaphor of family. Her worn physical form suggests the
life-draining effects of tenantry, and yet her generous nurturing sta-
bilizes the family. Agee thus far has presented Annie Mae as mother,
as George Gudger's wife, as half a couple, emphasizing that pairing
through the sleeping scenes. When he creates the first separate narrative of the text, however, the story of Emma's deciding whether or
not to follow her possessive and abusive husband, Agee manages to separate woman from mate as he keeps Annie Mae as central to Emma's
story as Emma is herself.

Emma's laments as she does decide to go are heard through walls
as she and Annie Mae "withdraw into rooms" and comfort each other.
Annie Mae "grieves for her, and for the loss of her to her own loneliness, for she loves her." Without the support of her older sister (i.e.,
sister-in-law), Emma as Agee draws her is surrounded by lust. She is
the sexual object and nothing else. Agee as character himself fanta-
sizes that one way to make Emma's coming life of relocation away
from family bearable is to give her complete sexual satiation: "if only

Emma could spend her last few days alive having a gigantic good time in bed, with George, a kind of man she is best used to, and with Walker and with me, whom she is curious about and attracted to. . . ." The choice of the modifier "alive" intensifies his hardly impartial view that Emma should stay with Annie Mae, whose wisdom as a sexual being allows her to blink at George's attraction to the younger woman. Surrounded with these marauding men, including the truck driver who is to drive her and her belongings away, Emma finally breaks— "got up, as suddenly as if she had to vomit, and went into the next room and shut the door, and Annie Mae followed her." Despite Agee the character's thinking that Emma "deserves" (has "earned"?) a "gigantic good time" sexually, Agee the narrator adds stroke after stroke to the image of Emma as Annie Mae/Annie Mae as Emma, the female principle, somehow suffusing the bleak life of the tenant family with that warmth and force it has. In his stress on the deep bond between the sisters, Agee leads the reader to identify one woman's plight as the other's. From what the text presents, George Gudger is not an abusive man, though he could be a wandering one; but the reader knows that any wife's role in a marriage, especially one lived in extreme poverty, is tenuous, as well as powerless.

Agee's suggestion that Gudger might be unfaithful seems at variance with the implied reasons for his choosing the Gudgers as the primary family in his account. True, theirs is the house in which he stayed. But they are also the youngest family and, for now, the most prosperous—and the most hopeful. (Treating the disillusioned Woodses as a lead family might have been a more powerful political statement, and the qualities of relative prosperity and hope might have argued against Agee's choosing the Gudgers.) But there may be another agenda in the choices made: the Gudgers are the most middle class in their behavior. It is the first marriage for both, and Annie Mae at least seems to have been romantically enthralled with the actual marriage, or so the later details about her bridal dress would suggest. Their children are all their children. And the eye—both human and camera—can still recognize the vestiges of Annie Mae's beauty and pride. Through her waning attractiveness the plight of the three tenant families becomes approachable, understandable.

But, once Agee has singled her out as the icon of the ravages of poverty and has aligned her with Emma in the role of sexual prey, he has begun the process of making the fiction of Annie Mae Gudger into a love story. Agee ennobles her, describes her situation, and suggests that she may lose her essential male support—and then, trained readers that we are, we await her "rescue." As Agee has constructed his narrative, the only means of rescue for Annie Mae is a male outsider: she has no education; she has children; she can hardly become self-supporting. Her rescue must come in the form of another love relationship.

The "subliminal" plot, the subtext of *Let Us Now Praise Famous Men*, then, is our waiting to see what will happen to Annie Mae, and that plot receives frequent substantiation: Annie Mae is often used as the prototype tenant farmer wife, to stand for the general experience. She is also the only one of the women to give voice and language—and tears—to her dissatisfaction about her home: "Oh, I do *hate* this house *so bad!* Seems like they ain't nothing in the whole world I can do to make it pretty" (210). When Agee moves into the catalogs of objects that blend Whitmanic catalogs with Steinian objectification (as in her *Tender Buttons*), many of the objects he describes are either Annie Mae's or her children's, and several of hers are either sexual ("A long homemade shift of coarse white cotton . . . a tincture of perspiration and of sex" [173]) or lush. Agee closes the chapter he has titled "Clothing" with the image of Annie Mae being married, wearing

> the great-brimmed, triumphal crown . . . reminiscent of the hats which were stylish around 1900. She was sixteen then; her skin would have been white, and clear of wrinkles, her body and its postures and her eyes even more pure than they are today; and she would have been happy, and confident enough in her beauty, to wear it without fear: and in her long white home made marriage dress and in that glory of a hat, with her sister Emma, seven years old, marveling up at her, and her mother standing away and approving her while her image slowly turned upon itself on blank floor and in a glass, she was such a poem as no human being shall touch. (286)

His reverence here, coupled with his admonition—again subliminal, Annie Mae as untouchable—is an ambivalent part of his strange excitement as he explores, and gives witness to, the Gudger house (a "tabernacle"), a process that recreates sexual excitement—even though he takes pains to deny that parallel, noting that "here there is no open sexual desire" (137). In Agee's role of narrator, he tries to explain the reactions of Agee the character—but he cannot explain away the admittedly sexual tension that unifies the disparate sections of the text. *Let Us Now Praise Famous Men* is engrossing, involving reading, taking the reader on and into the varied parts as if a taut plot line were in place. It is.

Most important in this narrative strategy is Agee's bringing the reader repeatedly to Annie Mae's "story" as sleeper. In one flashback to preparations for bed, he shows Emma and Annie Mae once again as one form ("the women, their plain shifts lifted from the closet nails, undress themselves, turned part away from each other, and careful not to look" [71]). She also appears as sensual woman ("infinitely tired, delicate animal"); as woman cut off from education, sent into work and marriage without choice ("On the day you are married, at about sixteen if you are a girl . . . a key is turned, with a sound not easily audible, and you are locked between the stale earth and the sky; the key turns in the lock behind you, and your full life's work begins, and there is nothing conceivable for which it can afford to stop short of your death, which is a long way off" [322–23]), and—perhaps most important—as one who already "loves" the character James Agee. He creates this latter identity very early, when—in the midst of the "Emma" narrative—he pictures the language-bereft Emma managing to say, passionately, to Agee (and it *is* to Agee; Walker is gone, though she asks him to share what she has said with Walker):

> Emma appeared, all dressed to go, looking somehow as if she had
> come to report a decision that had been made in a conference, for
> which I, without knowing it, seemed to have been waiting. She spoke in
> that same way too, not wasting any roundabout time or waiting for an
> appropriate rhythm, yet not in haste, looking me steadily and sweetly
> in the eyes, and said, I want you and Mr. Walker to know how much we
> all like you, because you make us feel easy with you; we don't have to
> act any different from what it comes natural to act, and we don't have
> to worry what you're thinking about us, it's just like you was our own
> people and had always lived here with us, you all are so kind, and nice,

and quiet, and easygoing, and we wisht you wasn't never going to go
away but stay on here with us, and I just want to tell you how much we
all keer about you; Annie Mae says the same. . . . (64)

Emma's direct, unembarrassed fluidity, speaking words she might
have chosen "in a conference"—a suggestion that Annie Mae and she
together decided what should be said—and closing with the reference
to her older sister's feelings ("how much we all keer about you") makes
clear the real situation. Because Emma is leaving, *she* can speak. She does
not have to face any consequences of her confession, for that is the
form in which she speaks. The human bonding that has occurred,
even though the reader finds it implausible—just as Agee surely did
as he lived in the household—to think they were comfortable with
him when he was so conscious that he was taking much-needed food
and small comforts from their daily lives—makes Emma feel unworthy of his kindness, surely a paradox to Agee as observer. But on the
other hand, if she is so conscious of their equality, if he has so well
played his part to make them understand their own value as human beings, regardless of their economic place, then a love between them—
either Emma or Annie Mae—is not implausible.

This sense of the plausibility of love, of caring both sexual and
asexual, suffuses Agee's text. It manages to link the almost lifeless
blocks of prose describing work, education, the shape of the house; it
brings the reader, still fascinated with unraveling the text, to the somehow inevitable culmination of the last sections. (We are reminded that
Agee wrote in a draft of the text, "The whole of the text is, loosely, an
experiment in sonata form, and is a two part song. . . . There are
other forms within these forms; related to those of motion pictures
as well as to those of music; and still other forms developed of numbers and of symbols. These, however, it seems better not to point out").[3]
Toward the end of *Let Us Now Praise Famous Men*, to complete the pat-
terning Agee has established in his unique stream-of-consciousness-of-
recall, a technique based obviously on different stages of recollection in
different kinds of memory, Agee settles the matter of his relationship
to Annie Mae Gudger in her role as romantic heroine. In what appears to be a strangely abrupt section of narrative, he depicts his separating from Evans—because each of them needs privacy, from each

other and from the work—and his fantasy of finding, as he puts it, "a piece of tail." His fantasy convinces him that he does not want any impersonal sexual experience so instead he finds a smaller southern town on this still heat-drenched Sunday (leaving Birmingham for Centerboro) and, in the context of the small town, recreates his first masturbatory experience, at age eleven, in his grandfather's empty house on a similar Sunday. From this vision, he performs another male ritual—confronting three adolescent boys in a dingy lunch-room, wishing he had some reason to fight them; and then imagining a girl to take to a hillside and make love with, a girl "nearly new" to him, a girl who "would have a good body in a thin white cotton dress" (382–88).

Returning to the very site he was trying to escape by driving into Birmingham, the land of the three tenant families, Agee finds himself in the Gudger house, drawn instinctively toward the most understandable of the three men, George Gudger. What Agee describes then, at the end of his narrative, *is* his first night within the Gudger house. As if drawn inescapably to that house and its repeated bedroom scene, lit by the flickering wick of the single lamp—Gudger, his children, and finally "you, Annie Mae, whose name I do not yet know, and whom I have never yet seen, and who I gather, are George's wife (though there has been no foolishness of 'introductions,' nor any word spoken, of any such kind): it is you I was first aware of from when first I came into this room, before you were yet a shadow out of the darkness, and you I have had on my mind while we have sat here, and so much cared toward, how from the first you not only never spoke but have not once lifted your face, your head, where you hold it there bowed deep . . ." (398). The erotic elements of Annie Mae's drawing Agee to her, the sharp, indelible physical attraction, completes the early sketch of Agee's growing friendship, love, caring, with the Gudger women; what Agee has evoked in his passionate description is the omnipresent, and genderless, fantasy of soul mate, love at first sight, people made for each other.

And the narrative promises to complete our expectations: Annie Mae rouses from her fear of the thunderstorm (though caught in that fear as she is, she becomes a child—her children pity her, and she becomes even more needful, a fit object for a lover's protection) and reclaims her baby boy from her oldest child, Louise, who has been playing the surrogate mother role. She has been playing the surrogate lover role with Agee as well, and he describes his feelings of "excitation" in some detail. When Louise transfers the baby to Annie Mae, so that she can feed him—modestly turning away from the visitor to do so—she also transfers the sexual flirtation she and Agee have been indulging in (a flirtation he describes as "such a vibration increasing between us as drove me half unconscious. . . . I with a qualifying protectiveness toward her from myself, she without fear nor wonder, but with extraordinary serene reception and shining and studiousness") (400–401).

After getting a meal for Agee, Annie Mae and her family go to bed, giving him the room the children usually sleep in. Surrounded by the smells and sounds of the family, his bed still warm from the formerly sleeping children, Agee surveys the room in which he finds himself. His sensory impression is that it is "thin-walled, skeletal, and beautiful . . . as if it were a little boat in the darkness," and he runs his fingers upon the wood "as it were skin" (421). Aroused, he opens the family bible to find the marriages and births of the Gudger family, and when he does lie back on the uncomfortable mattress, he smells "new blood" in his pillowcase and feels "little piercings and crawlings all along the surface of my body." His knowledge that the bed is infested comes after his fantasy: "I tried to imagine intercourse in this bed; I managed to imagine it fairly well," and then his quasi-sexual description of the bugs: "I lay awhile rolling and tightening against each new point of irritation. . . . To lie there naked feeling whole regiments of them tooling at me." As Agee kills the bugs and lice, smelling "their queer rankness," he begins to come to terms with the life he is learning. He goes outdoors for relief, feeling much "stronger than before, lawless and lustful to be naked" (426)—and, above all, reconciled.

In a text that purports to praise the workaday lives of the tenant farmers, and by extension the poor everywhere, *why* this long ending section on bedbugs and lice, and the minutely detailed discomfort of Agee the character's battle with them, as they continued "pricking and munching away . . . nibbling" (427)? It is as if the only way Agee can convince the reader of the physicality of such living is through

the physical response of his body itself. The section describes the
Gudgers' bed, as he learns his introduction to their lives without
anyone's using the word "introduce," through his body—accepting
the ironic reversal of the usual meanings of "pleasure" and "pain" in
his bedding-down experience with his all-too-animate bedfellows. He
concludes this section, "I don't exactly know why anyone should be
'happy' under these circumstances, but there's no use laboring the
point: I was: outside the vermin, my senses were taking in nothing
but a deep-night, unmeditatable consciousness of a world which was
newly touched and beautiful to me, and I must admit that even in
the vermin there was a certain amount of pleasure" (427–28).

The pleasure, Agee's earlier text suggests, accrues in part from
his bedroom's proximity to the Gudger family's sleeping space, the
arrangement so often previously described, centered in the matriar-
chal and erotic beauty of the Gudger wife. And therefore, predict-
ably, Agee ends his text with the descriptions of two images, disclaim-
ing all writerly responsibility for their existence. (The images describe
two of the Walker Evans photographs that appear as the first part of
the book; they are Agee's attempt to purify his account, to merge
back into the visual power that Evans's photos so graphically affect.)
The first is a depiction of Annie Mae's nursing the same baby boy
she was nursing at the end of the first night in Gudger's home, so
that this coda seems an extension, not a change from the writerly
text the reader has been following. The two figures are in the same
posture, but the act of nursing is, for the first time, given in great
detail, and the act of the child nursing becomes the act of sexual
arousal—the child is naked, he is unconsciously mimicking adult
love-making in his passion for food: "his hands are blundering at her
breast blindly . . . as if they were sobbing, ecstatic with love; his mouth
is intensely absorbed at her nipple as if in rapid kisses," and, as a result of his intense satisfaction, Agee reports, "his face is beatific, the
face of one at rest in paradise." The paragraph closes with one last
sensual detail, "the penis is partly erected" (441–42).

The last paragraph of Agee's carefully calculated coda is a description of the niece Ellen, she too completely at peace (like Annie
Mae's knees in the above description, "relaxed . . . her dress open
and one broken breast exposed"), her own less than two-year-old
body reflecting the vaginal power to complement the phallic, as Agee

describes it, "this center and source . . . a snoring silence of flame . . . a thing so strong, so valiant, so unvanquishable, I know it shall at length outshine the sun" (441, 442). The life force, whatever force Agee saw and revered in this culture and its people, became represented in the sexual. And to these people, Agee completes the circle of narrative, dedicating the book itself with the inscription: "To those of whom the record is made./In gratefulness and in love."

There is a wealth of paraphernalia as readers go into and come away from Agee's narrative (which he described in his notes as being "among other things, . . . an insult, a swindle, and a corrective").[4] Cynical appendages, notes, satiric answers to the 1939 *Partisan Review* authors' questionnaire, prayers, poems, pieces of Agee's memories and living that he hopes will fill the spaces, complement what he has brought himself to write. The story of the composition of this amazing piece of literature is already well known; what might not be as commonly understood is that, once Agee returned to the North and began the difficult and deliberately unintellectualized process of writing "a skeptical study of the nature of reality and of the false nature of recreation and of communication,"[5] his book became another of those inexplicable and unrepeatable American masterpieces, like Poe's *Eureka*, Thoreau's *Walden*, Melville's *Moby-Dick*, Hart Crane's *The Bridge*, Williams's *Paterson*, Dos Passos's *U.S.A.*, and of course Whitman's *Leaves of Grass*, and, like them, its definable and describable narrative is less the observable pattern than the undercurrents of thought and feeling that the unusual writing manages to express. My suggestion here is that some of the exquisite far-reaching quality of *Let Us Now Praise Famous Men* accrues from Agee's shaping his love of the tenant farmers in the form of a classic romantic fable: giving his love for them a sexual dimension that enthralls, arouses, and convinces the reader.

Agee's strange text does, indeed, do what he had hoped—and what he had described in his 1937 "Plans for Work": "It is to be as exhaustive a reproduction and analysis of personal experience, including the phases and problems of memory and recall and revisitation and the problems of writing and of communication, as I am capable of, with constant bearing on two points: to tell everything possible as accurately as possible; and to invent nothing. It involves therefore as total a suspicion of 'creative' and 'artistic' as of 'reportorial' attitudes and methods, and it is likely therefore to involve the development of some more or less new forms of writing and of observation."[6] And it did that to the extent that readers fifty years later are still puzzling over the moving, challenging, enervating, and erotic experience that reading Agee's work becomes.

## Notes

1. James Agee and Walker Evans, *Let Us Now Praise Famous Men* (Boston: Houghton, 1941), 13. This edition will be cited parenthetically hereafter in text.
2. Walt Whitman's "The Sleepers" includes such relevant lines as these: "I wander all night in my vision, / Stepping with light feet . . . swiftly and noiselessly stepping and stopping, / Bending with open eyes over the shut eyes of sleepers; / The married couple sleep calmly in their bed, he with his palm on the hip of the wife, and she with her palm on the hip of the husband / The sisters sleep lovingly side by side in their bed, / The men sleep lovingly side by side in theirs, / And the mother sleeps with her little child carefully wrapped / The sleepers are very beautiful as they lie unclothed, / Learned and unlearned are hand in hand . . . and male and female are hand in hand." *Harper American Literature*, vol. 1 (New York: Harper, 1987), 2390, 2396.
3. James Agee, "Notes and Appendix" section of draft manuscript of *Let Us Now Praise Famous Men*, 354, Agee Collection, Harry Ransom Humanities Center, University of Texas, Austin. Used by permission of the Humanities Center.
4. James Agee, sidebound notebook labeled "Let Us Now Praise Famous Men," n.p., Agee Collection, Harry Ransom Humanities Center, University of Texas, Austin.
5. James Agee, "Plans for Work: October, 1937," in *Collected Short Prose of James Agee*, ed. Robert Fitzgerald (Boston: Houghton, 1969), 134.
6. Ibid., 133.

# Prophet from Highland Avenue: Agee's Visionary Journalism

## *Paul Ashdown*

THE FEAST OF THE TRANSFIGURATION, 1945. A bomb sunders the universe and places in mortal hands a power so enormous that now "reason and spirit meet on final ground."[1] That raiment, white and glistening, once seen on a holy mountain near Jerusalem, covers Hiroshima like a shroud, and James Agee turns to the Forty-ninth Psalm for consolation.

He writes for *Time* magazine "a kind of editorial" at the behest of a bishop's son, his editor T. S. Matthews, who, like Agee, is a child of the Episcopal church.[2] He speaks with the prophetic voice:

> When the bomb split open the universe and revealed the prospect of the infinitely extraordinary, it also revealed the oldest, simplest, commonest, most neglected and most important of facts: that each man is eternally and above all else responsible for his own soul, and, in the terrible words of the Psalmist, that no man may deliver his brother, nor make agreement unto God for him.[3]

In *Elegant Jeremiahs*, George P. Landow argues that Victorian sages such as John Ruskin, Matthew Arnold, and Thomas Carlyle established a vital Anglo-American nonfiction literary genre. He cites Carlyle's "Signs of the Times" as the first fully developed example of the genre. He suggests that portions of the work of some important contemporary journalists—specifically Tom Wolfe, Joan Didion, and Norman Mailer—may fall within this genre and contends that certain works of contemporary nonfiction, including autobiography, may be better understood as contributions to the genre.

Landow's Victorian sage, writing in a genre derived from biblical prophecy and apocalyptics with occasional metaphoric infusion from classical mythology, speaks as an outsider, a doughty critic of the way things are or of inimical social forces that changed the way things were. He conceives of this sage, or prophet, after T. H. Huxley and others, as *forthspeaker* rather than *foreteller* of events.

As heirs to the tradition, he argues, twentieth-century prophets sometimes depart from the Victorians but still are likely to be both satirical and visionary, to both attack and inspire their readers and to seek meaning in ostensibly trivial or grotesque events. They, too, seek to restore the powers of language, to warn of impending dangers, and to define what is human and what is not in an age of technology. They are more likely to seek credibility by confessing their inadequacies than by claiming divine sanction. And, in a time of moral and intellectual relativism, they often hesitate to claim certain knowledge or to attempt to speak from authority. Yet they repeatedly try to persuade the audience, usually episodically rather than through carefully structured arguments, that they are percipient and reliable observers who must not be ignored.[4]

Landow cautions that the sage "may have strange progeny or stepchildren, and one cannot fully appreciate the importance of the works in this genre until one tracks them all down and discovers all the ways in which the words of these elegant Jeremiahs take form and the possibly strange and unexpected effects they produce."[5] The works of many modern American literary figures included within genres frequently, and imprecisely, called "documentary," "literary journalism," and "New Journalism" might, upon closer examination, fit into Landow's taxonomy.[6] Theodore Dreiser, John Hersey, and Ernest Hemingway, for example, might be described as prophetic writers. But because few modern writers have been as earnestly prophetic as James Agee in so many forms of writing—poetry, novels, criticism, screenplays, journalism, short stories, autobiography and letters—he could be considered foremost among the "strange progeny" Landow seeks to track down.

From 1932 through the early 1950s, Agee produced a remarkable body of forthspeaking journalism that discerned, in the tradition of Carlyle, the signs of the times. His prophetic writings told of the division and fragmentation of modern American life, its indifference to land and the people who tilled it, and its growing industrial arrogance, culminating in the atomic bomb. Agee called the kind of prophetic writing he wanted to do "the directest, most incisive and specific, and angriest possible form of direct address, semi-scientic, semi-religious; set in terms of the greatest available human intensity."[7] He envisioned pieces of writing "whose rough parallel is the prophetic writings of the Bible."[8]

His most revealing attempt to define the terms of his prophetic address is to be found in "Dedication," a prose-poem that appeared in *Permit Me Voyage*, a collection of his verse published in October 1934.[9] The poet Robert Fitzgerald, a close friend of Agee's who is among the pantheon of artists (Hemingway, Joyce, Fitzgerald, et al.) named in "Dedication," saw *Permit Me Voyage* as "the work of a desperate Christian" and "Dedication" as a strenuous prayer.[10] Alfred T. Barson contends that, while Agee intended to write "Dedication" in the "generalized and impersonal tone of the Litany or General Supplication" from *The Book of Common Prayer*, the work is "closer to the stridency" of Jeremiah and Isaiah. Barson argues that "Dedication" is a moral statement by which Agee attempts to subordinate what he called "all things as you loved and detested them" to "the prophetic mission he conceived as poetry."[11]

As a student at Harvard, Agee wrote a poem about prophecy for *The Harvard Advocate*. Called "Good Friday," the poem begins:

> High in Dodona's swaying groves
> High in the grey, the glimmering oaks,
> Dodona's cauldrons, convolute,
> Groan on the wind strange prophecies.[12]

Dodona is thought to have been a grove of sacred oaks at Epirus, where Zeus was revered. Thunderstorms were said to occur there more frequently than elsewhere in Europe. Priests and priestesses drew oracles by interpreting the sound of the wind rustling the branches and vessels of brass in the trees and the murmuring of a sacred spring that gushed from the roots of a great oak.[13] Agee's poem has Pan hearing a prophecy of the coming of Christ and being crucified himself against two trees in the grove. Milton, Tennyson, Cowper, and Elizabeth Barrett Browning addressed the theme in different ways.[14] Carlyle used Dodona as a metaphor for the prophecies of Coleridge.[15]

As a child in Knoxville, Tennessee, Agee, then called Rufus, had first wondered "who shall ever tell the sorrow of being on this earth." When he tried to recall the intuitions of childhood in the 1940s as he was writing an autobiographical novel, published posthumously in 1957 as *A Death in the Family*, he described himself as a six-year-old boy listening to the sound of the wind in the trees outside his bedroom window on Highland Avenue in 1916.

> The light put the shadows of moving leaves against the curtains. . . . Without touching each other these leaves were stirred as, silently, the whole tree moved in its sleep. . . .
> He heard the summer night.
> All the air vibrated like a fading bell. . . .
> Darkness said:
> When is this meeting, child, where are we, who are you child . . . do you know who you are . . . ?
> He knew that he would never know. . . . That yet in that desolation, he was not without companions. For featureless on the abyss, invincible, moved monstrous intuitions.[16]

Now what were these "monstrous intuitions," these "strange prophecies" he heard or imagined in the rustling of the leaves of trees? He put into the mind of the child a certain prescience about his father's death. In the novel, Rufus and his father walk downtown "in the light of mother-of-pearl" after supper to see a Charlie Chaplin film at the Majestic Theater on Gay Street. On the way home, Rufus senses their mutual dependence, but that very night his father is called to the side of his own father in the mountains north of Knoxville, a journey from which he never returns.[17] Hugh James Agee was killed in an automobile accident near Knoxville on May 18, 1916, and his son grieved over his loss throughout his life.

Richard N. Owen rented a room from Agee's mother shortly after the accident when he was a student at the University of Tennessee. He recalls that Rufus was "greatly affected by his father's death and was crying all the time." Owen at that time was in the Students Army Training Corps and drilled regularly on the University of Tennessee campus a few blocks away. He recalled that a Marine recruiting officer was also residing in the Agee home.[18] The child Rufus could have had little awareness of the war in Europe, but the mature Agee, recalling the presence of soldiers in his home, possibly coupled the coming of war to the child's prescience. His father's death came only six weeks before the slaughter of the Somme battles, and direct American involvement in the conflict came within a year.

Even more ironic is the lyrical prologue to *A Death in the Family*, "Knoxville: Summer 1915," with its celebration of selfless familial love and the crepuscular sounds of summer set against the keening dissonance of war and the coming tragedy. The site of Agee's home at 1505 Highland Avenue is now occupied by the Fountain Place Condominiums, "fenced for privacy, and guarded with dawn-to-dusk security."[19]

For the rest of his childhood, Agee clung precariously to an intensely guilt-ridden, precocious religious faith largely imposed on him by his devoutly Anglo-Catholic mother. He was taken to a boarding school run by Episcopal monks in the Cumberland Mountains of Tennessee, but at the age of twelve he had a spiritual crisis that left him "through with religion but still carrying a deep load of it, some of it benign, much of it poisonous." In its place was a strong "gravitation toward death."[20] An Exeter classmate recalls that as a schoolboy Agee was "inwardly scratched with anguish."[21]

When Agee hitchhiked from Harvard to New York for a job with Henry Luce's *Fortune* magazine in 1932, he was still a troubled and troubling young man. Before him lay the city he had first seen at the age of fifteen, when he had "walked in the late brilliant June dusk into the blinding marvel of Times Square . . . my heart nearly breaking for joy here where all the shows of every kind on the otherwise rural round planet were spread at once before me, a giant tray of choiring diamonds."[22]

But at twenty-two he was "settling into despair of everything I want and everything about myself. If I am, as I seem to be, dying on my feet mentally and spiritually, and can do nothing about it, I'd prefer not to know I was dying."[23] He had been contemplating suicide, and with true melancholic angst, proclaimed that the "whole spiritual tone of this time seems the darkest and saddest in centuries."[24]

*Fortune* was a curious place for him to work out his own salvation. Founded in 1928 as a new kind of business magazine that would both celebrate American capitalism and tenderly probe its weaknesses, *Fortune* had attracted a stable of superb writers who were hardly sympathetic to their subject matter. Eric Hodgins, a managing editor, said he thought *Fortune* had "the most brilliant magazine staff ever to exist in America" in spite of the staff being "insane, unreliable and alcoholic." Before Agee's arrival, the magazine's editor had flung himself, stark naked, to his death off the roof of a building.[25] Agee himself later contemplated plunging from his office on the fifty-second floor of the Chrysler Building to the street below.[26]

Although Agee "sat in his office and sucked on the end of his pencil for so long after he was hired" that his mentor, Archibald MacLeish, was afraid he would be fired, he soon distinguished himself on a number of assignments.[27] These included moralistic assessments of the Tennessee Valley Authority, Roman society under Fascism, horseracing at Saratoga, the commercial orchid industry, cockfighting, pollution, a cruise ship, and other topics from which he extrapolated odd and original insights in often stunning prose.

In these stories we begin to hear "monstrous intuitions" and "strange prophecies" that would seem to fulfill Landow's criteria for the twentieth-century sage. In most of them, some sort of death is in progress. An Italian prince quietly waits for death "in his marble-skinned and magnificent and cold palazzo." Gamecocks "can imagine no happier paradise than one in which rages an endless free-for-all, ending constantly in death." The Tennessee Valley Authority must move the graves of pioneer settlers including Agee's own ancestors and reconcile their descendants to a new way of life. "In this enormous machine," he writes, "the balance wheel is human."

In his Carlylean essay on smoke, he likens industrial effusions to "the breath of a collective beast, the breath of our time: foul, sterile, baneful to the things we cherish . . . and engendered by our civilization everywhere, like a curse that some obscure and nameless god might have laid upon us. . . ."[28] The greenhouse effect and other ecological disasters lay in the future, and the beast slouches onward, bringing new terrors.

An extraordinary essay, "The Great American Roadside," illustrates his broadest use of the prophetic voice. The assignment began in the summer of 1934 when Agee's editor, Ralph Ingersoll, had "a real honey of an article idea." He wanted to send Agee out on the roads and highways springing up throughout the country to accommodate the increasing volume of automobile traffic.[29] Karal Ann Marling speculates that the assignment owed its inspiration to Sinclair Lewis's 1928 novella *The Man Who Knew Coolidge*. The novella places the redoubtable George Babbitt in the position of learning from his friend Lowell Schmaltz about the roadside kitsch awaiting him along his proposed vacation route. Marling suggests that *Fortune* may have wondered what effect the Great Depression was having on the roadside economy.[30] Agee was more than up to the assignment. During the summer of 1929 he had hitchhiked across the country to find work in the fields. With impeccable credentials as a bourgeois tramp, he wrote stories about his adventures in *The Harvard Advocate*.[31]

If Agee glanced upward as he walked through the Chrysler Building lobby on his way to the open road, he would again have noticed on its ceiling the world's largest mural, a celebration of transportation, power, and technology culminating in this splendid cathedral of the automobile. Light poured through etched glass above three magnificent entrances and illuminated the variegated red Moroccan marble walls.[32] Below, revolving on a turntable, was a glistening 1934 Chrysler Airflow, an eight-cylinder, five-passenger, aerodynamic sedan, hardly at all like the brass-nosed, black 1915 Model T Ford that Agee's father had driven off a rural road eighteen years earlier.[33]

The fatal accident had been caused, in part, by a difficult stretch of descending, unpaved road that forked abruptly over a narrow bridge near the site of a Civil War skirmish. The road was not unlike most others of its time, especially in the Southern Appalachians, but within two decades some 900,000 miles of "hard-fleshed highway" stretched across the country and the automobile had become the driving wheel of the American economy.[34] While the automobile was remaking the landscape, creating suburban villages out of forests, fields, and pastures, huge amounts of capital were required to accommodate the necessary commercial and infrastructural changes. The automobile helped create the prosperity of the 1920s and then helped drive the country straight into the Great Depression.[35]

But the Great Depression was, if anything, hastening the great migrations that were occurring on the vast highway system, activating the wanderlust that had been a part of the American character since before the wagon trains. Writers from Whitman to Twain to Hemingway had in some measure celebrated the American road, but Agee was chary of what he saw as contemporary sentimentality about tourism and the American pioneer spirit. He sensed that Americans found in motion a counterfeit form of the empirical knowledge that comes from purposeful travel. The historian Frederick Lewis Allen suggested in 1952 that the automobile had suited the American genius. "For that genius was not static but venturesome; Americans felt that a rolling stone gathers experience, adventure, sophistication, and—with luck—new and possibly fruitful opportunities."[36]

For two months Agee watched "the spreaded swell and swim of the hard highway toward and beneath and behind and gone and the parted roadside swarming past," documenting what he saw and thinking about the story.[37] Agee wrote furiously for weeks after his return until Ingersoll snatched eight thousand words off the top of his desk one evening and sent them to the printer. Agee, unaware of the larceny, continued writing until Hodgins told him the story was already in galleys.[38] It contained many elements of the prophetic voice suggested by Landow.

Agee begins the story by stating and then exaggerating the human scale of what he has observed: "by very considerable odds the greatest road the human race has ever built . . . incomparably the most hugely extensive market the human race has ever set up to tease and tempt and take money from the human race . . . a new way of life, a new but powerfully established American institution." The road is at once both a great technological and democratic triumph and a means by which those who built the road will become victims of predation and exploitation. The human thus becomes conjoined with the anti-human. The road's true purposes are ambiguous, elusive, "not well defined." But the purposes of the roadside are clear. The roadside is organic, inseparable from the whole organism: the continent, the people, the automobile, the road and the roadside, and "the ultimate expression of the conspiracy that produced it."

The reader is buffeted by the sage's jibes. Certain facts the readers know, but their significance "may never have sharply occurred" to them. The word *sharply* is indicative of the tone of the attack, which progresses with the admonition that even if the reader is aware of "these things as they are, it isn't likely that you know just why they grew so fast, just why they are as they are." The reader is further afflicted by the claim that "few" Americans know much about themselves, implying that all must attend as the prophet enlightens them.

Agee finds the American people racially restless, restive "entirely for the sake of restiveness." They move about for no reason, like nomadic tribes that have lost sight of their covenant. Exposed in the wilderness, they leave themselves open to their enemies, and the instrument of their destruction is the automobile. He introduces the automobile in a parody of the Book of Genesis: "So God made the American restive. The American in turn and in due time got into the automobile and found it good." Like forbidden fruit, the automobile at first satisfies the hunger for freedom but then sharpens that same desire for even greater mobility. Ultimately the automobile becomes a "hypnosis," becomes "the opium of the American people," leaving them malleable, bemused and comatose. A circle is completed, and it will "whirl for pleasure and for profit as long as the American blood and the American car are so happily married."

Then the sage moves to distinguish himself from lesser prophets, the satirists who merely ridicule the roadside. They fail to see that the phenomenon is not merely derisory but exists because the city, with its costly and often disreputable hotels, interrupts and delays travel. The new sojourners "have money to spend but not on the marble foyers of their forefathers. Their money is dedicated to motion. . . ." The road provides a functional alternative to the hotel: the cabin camp. The camp succeeds because it is simple and efficient, a sound contribution to the American landscape although its destiny is uncertain.

Agee finds meaning in the grotesque. He finds a tourist cabin that has been converted from a rabbit hutch and a hen house in a camp gussied up by petunias and a tawdry rock garden. He satirizes the owners of the camps, who survive by trying to run subsidiary businesses while tending to their clientele. He finds "signs and portents" of their future in legislation intended to regulate them and raise their standards. He sees in these laws the hand of the hotel owners who fear competition from the camps but predicts that the improvements will ultimately doom the hotels by making the camps even more attractive to the middle class.

When he makes a specific prediction about the future, he confesses his lack of prescience and his uncertainty. He doubts that the camps will be replaced by chain-owned and standardized establishments as they, of course, ultimately were, and he misreads the basic economic advantages of centralized management. But he clearly understands the essential fact: "that more and more powerfully, the habit is upon us to refuel and eat and sleep and amuse ourselves not in the towns as towns—they slow us up—but along the open roadside which is a new kind of town itself, and in the little towns that have all but turned themselves into roadsides."

And along these roadsides the sage points to an infinite variety of commercialized caves with their fraudulently named lakes and chambers, stands offering trinkets and debased foods, institutional icons and grotesque colossi. He acknowledges their appeal as popular and ostensibly innocent attractions but reminds the reader that their purpose is predatory and narcissistic, their solicitations counterfeit and their appeal unwholesome. He concludes with a warning that the traveler, now emblematically described as an "autoist," reacts "delicately to the wonders of this land out of the midst of his easy coma" in ways revealing the inner mind.[39]

Highway historian Warren James Belasco acknowledges the popularity of Agee's essay. He notes that, during a time of class unrest, the road had indeed provided a powerful image of unity. But Belasco points out that this imagery also served, perhaps ironically, as good public relations for the automobile industry.[40] Projecting these observations a half century and more into the future, we can note with recognition the national gridlock on the highways, the continuing destruction of the cities, and the voracious commercialization of the roadside in ways Agee could hardly have imagined.

Despite the freedom he enjoyed to write such prophetic essays,

Agee grew increasingly restless and cynical as a *Fortune* staff writer. He later complained of his "three years of exposure to foulness" as he continued to demonstrate his ability to venture into the country-side and find meaning in ordinary events.[41]

"Saratoga" discloses the dark side of the horse racing industry, which brought the well heeled to the Adirondacks for recreation pro-vided by gamblers and prostitutes. A law that prohibited bookies from openly soliciting at the race track had been repealed in 1934, and Agee closely observed their tactics with the wry insight of a Damon Runyon. In order to attract off-season business, Franklin Roosevelt, as governor of New York, had encouraged development of the springs at Saratoga as a spa. But the city saw little new business because the newly mobile middle-class motorists were not inclined to spend months loll-ing indolently beside the waters as the wealthy had done for decades. It was too easy for them to get to Saratoga on the new highways and just as easy for them to move on when they grew restless. Saratoga is really just another terminus on the Great American Roadside.[42] When the racing season ends, all that is left in the city is "the chill and the very temper and the very cold of death," Agee's familiar metaphor for the age.[43] And by 1951, another Tennessean, U.S. Senator Estes Kefauver, was paying attention to the Saratoga gamblers. His televised Senate crime-committee hearings exposed the mobsters who con-trolled the gambling and prostitution rackets and brought about re-forms that impeded their trade. Saratoga was never the same.[44]

Taken as a whole, Agee's articles form a codex filled with cryptic warnings, often satirical, usually ominous. But what he really wanted was an opportunity to step outside his text and to comment directly on its actual significance. To do this he needed a project that would enable him to operate on a larger stage. The opportunity came sud-denly in the spring of 1936 when Ingersoll asked him if he would like to return to the South to write an article about tenant farming. Agee was "stunned, exalted, scared clean through."[45] When he returned to New York at the end of a two-month trip through the South with the photographer Walker Evans, his notebooks contained the elements of what would become *Let Us Now Praise Famous Men,* one of the great prophetic books of the twentieth century.

*Fortune*'s rejection of Agee's manuscript, its eventual publication by Houghton Mifflin in 1941, its subsequent commercial failure, and its rediscovery in 1960 after the success of *A Death in the Family* in 1957, have become a piece of literary folklore. *Let Us Now Praise Famous Men* has itself been much praised, variously interpreted, sometimes dismissed by unregenerate critics. Considered as a book of predictions, the work has limited utility. But understood as prophetic writing in the tradition of Landow's modern sage, the book stands as a stunning example of forthspeaking journalism.

At its narrative level, *Let Us Now Praise Famous Men* is the story of three tenant families living in Hale County, Alabama, in the middle of the Great Depression. There is little direct quotation in *Let Us Now Praise Famous Men*, but the book is actually full of voices. The tenants speak obliquely as the prophetic voices of the priests and priestesses of Dodona. They are especially garrulous in their silences, communicating more by their countenances and their primitive intuitions than by their voices. As a piece of straight reportage, the book attempts to explain cotton tenantry less as an economic phenomenon than as a problem in human divinity. The book is as much a theological or teleological treatise as it is sociology or economic history. The real villain in the book is journalism itself. In a poem written for Walker Evans, Agee calls the two journalists "spies, moving delicately among the enemy," and the poem goes on to invoke the patronage of the mad King Lear, who finally wanted to take on the mystery of things as if he were a spy in the service of God.[46]

But Agee and Evans were spies in the service of Henry Luce and *Fortune* magazine, exploiting the misery of human beings for profit. In a sense, it is as if King Lear wrote the book, and the content could be summarized as: "*Howl Howl Howl.*" Agee felt that as journalists they were expected to write not about people with immortal souls but about people who were members of broad statistical categories. He felt they had no right to intrude on the lives of naked helpless wretches, nor did they have any right to call them naked helpless wretches.

Another bit of irony lies in Time Inc., *Fortune*'s parent company, subsequently becoming Time-Warner, the world's largest print and entertainment conglomerate. Time-Warner is in limited partnership with Whittle Communications, which has its headquarters in Knoxville across the street from St. John's Cathedral, the church in which Agee was baptized. When plans for the firm's new headquarters were unveiled in 1986, owner Chris Whittle told the press the complex would be topped by "James Agee–style writing garrets."[47]

Throughout the book, Agee assumes the prophetic posture by denouncing his reader's unworthiness, his own inability to respond to what he sees or to explain his mission ("just say, I am from Mars, and let it go at that"), and the corruption inherent in any act of passively observing the misfortunes of others.[48] Masses of facts are presented, but these are used primarily to show the limitations of language and traditional reportage. As in "The Great American Roadside," the reader's understanding of facts is challenged: "To grasp such facts, to try to understand them and their application, would seem as primal and as relevant to and influential upon the rest of what we are and do as breathing. Our own inability to grasp them or our negligence, which amounts to the same thing, does not qualify us very highly to handle more difficult facts which are of central importance. . . ."[49]

When trivial objects used by the tenants are described, they serve to draw the reader into the sanctity of existence and to assist the sage in forthspeaking. There is, for example, a long discussion of an oil lamp by whose light the sage may, in respectful silence, "tell you anything within realm of God, whatsoever it may be, that I wish to tell you. . . ."[50]

At another level, the sage confesses that he is completing an autobiographical pilgrimage into the sources of his own existence: "And so in this quiet introit and in all the time we have stayed in this house, and in all we have sought, and in each detail of it, there is so keen, sad, and precious a nostalgia as I can scarcely otherwise know; a knowledge of brief truancy into the sources of my life, whereto I have no rightful access, having paid no price beyond love and sorrow."[51]

Along the way, the sage encounters grotesques, like shadow figures dredged up from the subconscious. "The older man came up suddenly behind me, jamming my elbow with his concave chest and saying fiercely *Awnk, awnk,* while he glared at me with enraged and terrified eyes. . . . The woman spoke to him sharply though not unkindly . . . as if he were a dog masturbating on a caller, and he with-

drew against a post of the porch and sank along it to the floor with
his knees up sharp and wide apart and the fingers of his left hand
jammed as deep as they would go down his gnashing mouth. . . ."[52]

The theme of exploitation and a warning about the future are
couched in a pre-Orwellian porcine analogy: "What would we have
to think of hogs who, having managed to secure justice among themselves, still and continuously and without the undertone of a thought
to the contrary exploited every other creature and material of the
planet, and who wore in their eyes, perfectly undisturbed by any second consideration, the high and holy light of science or religion."[53]

A central concern is the question of how we are to respond to
the plight of the tenant farmer. Writers of the 1930s had made the
tenant farmer a symbol of the national malaise. Many of their accounts
had brutally exploited the degrading conditions in which many of the
tenants lived. Agee wanted nothing to do with this kind of writing
and suspected the motives of publications such as *Fortune* that commissioned such articles. In his view, "the comfortable have always
been able to lick their chops over the hunger of others if that hunger is presented with the right sort of humorous or pathetic charm."[54]
He abhorred the voyeurism he thought this kind of reporting en-
tailed.

William Stott calls *Let Us Now Praise Famous Men* "a book of doom
and desperate resignation."[55] Stott finds that nearly all the reviewers
of the book's 1960 edition agreed that Agee had proved unreliable
as a social prophet. In the spirit of the era, the assumption was that
massive federal spending programs, the Second World War, and the
postwar prosperity had provided some hope for the tenants and had
lifted many of them out of poverty. But Stott argues from a 1973 perspective that Agee was not far off the mark and that the "doom Agee
foresaw has been largely realized."[56] Actually, rural poverty declined
until 1973, but then conditions began to worsen again.

Dale Maharidge and Michael Williamson visited Alabama in 1986
to find out what had become of Agee's tenants and their descendants. They concluded that Agee was overly pessimistic; the lives of
many of the tenants had improved, and they were as a class not devoid of hope. Sharecropping had not endured as an economic system of exploitation as Agee believed it would. But Maharidge and

Williamson acknowledged that most of the tenants remained in pre-
carious circumstances, vulnerable to economic recessions and unable
to draw much succor from periods of national prosperity. The decline of sharecropping had caused terrific economic and social upheavals. And the individual stories these authors uncovered held little
reason for optimism. As Agee predicted, the tenants faced a dismal
future, and Maharidge and Williamson, if anything, turned up more
grotesques, dreary landscapes and despair than Agee and Evans found a
half century before them. The land the tenants worked is now so bar-
ren it seems "some terrible holocaust must have claimed them."[57]

After returning from Alabama, Agee continued writing for *Fortune* but soon began reviewing books and films for *Time* and *The Nation*. W. H. Auden's much quoted letter to the editors of *The Nation*
praises Agee's film reviews as being of "profound interest, expressed
with such extraordinary wit and felicity." He says Agee's articles be-
long "in that very select class . . . of newspaper work which has per-
manent literary value."[58] Agee surely valued the compliment and recognized a kindred sage; a few months earlier he had described a
scene in a film as having "the sinister, freezing beauty of an Auden
prophecy come true."[59]

Agee used *The Nation* columns as forums for his social criticism.
They are especially notable for his skepticism about the presentation
of the war to the American public, calling the "well-paid shamming
of forms of violence and death which millions a day are meeting . . .
of an order more dubious than the shamming of all other forms of
human activity."[60] He said in 1945 that he was "beginning to believe
that, for all that may be said in favor of our seeing these terrible
records of war, we have no business seeing this sort of experience
except through our presence and participation." By watching war
films, he said, "we may be quite as profoundly degrading ourselves
and, in the process betraying and separating ourselves the farther
from those we are trying to identify ourselves with. . . ."[61]

One of his most powerful war essays suggests a Carlylean treatise
on power. He observes that Franklin Roosevelt, upon returning from
the Yalta conference, was profoundly changed, his countenance becoming "the face of a religious, even of a seer. . . . I felt in the face an
intimacy with death and with tragedy which I had never seen in it

before. . . ." Agee thought that, if a person as close to political agnos-
ticism as he was could "be moved by such a man, and such an event,
that may be one more measure and one more expression of what the
man and the event mean to those who have and who practice political hope and faith."

Finding it "hard to imagine that history can ever have brought
any man into a more terrible predicament" than the new president,
Harry Truman, Agee says that the existence of great men such as
Roosevelt did not shake his belief that "the best that is in any ordinary man is illimitable." Conflict, he believes, will strengthen not only
Truman but all ordinary men "because sympathy, responsibility, love,
magnanimity, resoluteness and the obligation to selflessness, now
more clearly than before, rest with great and equal weight upon all
human beings who can so much as apprehend their existence." He
argues that, to a great extent, "one is forced to fall back on a metaphysical yet very literal faith in unanimity and massiveness of spirit. I
believe that this exists, and that if it is known to exist it can have very
great power."[62]

Nevertheless, he felt the postwar world was going to be severely
tested by the splitting of the atom, which he saw as the great symbolic event of the century. As early as 1943, he deplored the intensifying schizophrenia which he believed was especially prevalent in the
United States, isolated as it was from the fighting that was being done
in other parts of the world. While other peoples were coming of age,
Americans, "a peculiarly neurotic people," remained "untouched, vir-
ginal, prenatal," and would emerge from the war "almost as if it had
never taken place."[63]

Propagandistic films would "demolish one's moral and aesthetic
judgment by splitting both and by turning the split forces of both
against each other."[64] When the bomb was finally dropped, Agee
mocked those who believed that "transcontinental commuting, better complexions, and the millennium itself will be achieved on the
power generated from an old hat check" and thought atomic energy
was, at its core, a monstrously egotistical enterprise.[65] Drawing imagery from his *Time* essay on the dropping of the bomb, he wrote in
1947 that reason involves "not merely the forebrain but the entire

being," residing in the ability "to recognize oneself, and others, primarily as human beings, and to recognize the ultimate absoluteness
of responsibility of each human being," nothing less than the essential argument of the Forty-ninth Psalm.[66]

Within Agee's film criticism are numerous prophecies about the
present and the coming age:

*On "the ghastly gelatinous nirvana" of television:* "In another fifty years—or
ten, I am willing to bet—moving pictures will no longer be the central
medium. Radio will have taken their place: television, very likely, will
have taken the place of both."[67]

*On the next generation:* "These girls may be no worse than the teen-age
girls of any other country, class, or generation, but I would be sorry to
believe that, and am sorrier still to imagine their children."[68]

*On cinema:* ". . . American films will become, more than ever before,
vapid, safe advertisements of our well-known way of life—even touched
up or supervised, perhaps, by the State Department; and . . . European
films will become more and more 'American' in style and content."[69]

*On war propaganda:* "Conditioned by such amphibious and ambiguous
semi-information, we are still more likely than otherwise to do things
to defeated enemies which, both morally and materially, will finally
damage us more deeply even than them."[70]

*On certain American types:* ". . . their chief preoccupations—blackmail
and what's-in-it-for-me—all seem to me to reflect . . . things that are
deeply characteristic of this civilization."[71]

*On the American character:* "Few Americans either behind or in front of
our cameras give evidence of any recognition or respect for themselves
or one another as human beings, or have any desire to be themselves
or to let others be themselves. On both ends of the camera you find
very few people who are not essentially, instead, just promoters, little
racketeers, interested in 'the angle.' I suspect it will some day be
possible to deduce out of our non-fiction films alone that the suppos-
edly strongest nation on earth collapsed with such magical speed
because so few of its members honored any others, or even themselves,
as human beings."[72]

*On liberty:* ". . . a terrifying number of Americans, most of them in all innocence of the fact, are much more ripe for benevolent dictatorship—and every dictatorship is seen as benevolent by those who support it—than for the most elementary realization of the meanings, hopes, and liabilities of democracy."[73]

*On evil:* ". . . practically nobody thinks it civilized, or in the interests of the common weal, to believe that there is such a thing as evil any more. . . ."[74]

*On democracy:* "I believe that a democracy which cannot contain all its enemies, of whatever kind or virulence, is finished as a democracy."[75]

*On Stalin's Soviet Union:* "More elaborate than any others they have developed a science of contempt for present humanity, including themselves in their own scruples as individuals, in the name of future humanity, and a science for utilizing, and conquering, those who believe merely in each other, or merely in self-advantage."[76]

*On the Cold War:* ". . . the real crucial conflict is not between the Stalinists and the nominal democracies. It is between those who honor existence and so, necessarily, morality and those who honor either only in the hypothetical future, if at all."[77]

*On Western Civilization:* "I doubt that it will continue. It has been rotting above ground, on its feet, legally classified as alive, for a long while already, and will destroy itself either by failure to shut out enough of its enemies, or by definitively violating its own nature in its primordial efforts to defend itself, or by shutting out, along with some of the more conspicuous of its enemies, all those who might conceivably preserve within it some last flicker of humanistic sanity."[78]

*On humanism:* "I realize that I must be exaggerating when I think of it as hardly existing in a pure and vigorous form anywhere in contemporary art or living, but I doubt that I am exaggerating much."[79]

But it is in the nature of prophecy to much exaggerate the dangers of the present, and Agee's gloomy social assessments and predictions were intended to arouse a deluded, apathetic public. The cinema, with its challenge to distinguish reality from fantasy, provided the forum he needed to make explicit the less accessible warnings he had sounded in his poetry, his more circumspect magazine writing, and the self-absorbing rage of *Let Us Now Praise Famous Men*. Those works, his film and television scripts, and his letters would be discovered by a wider audience only after Agee's death and the triumph of *A Death in the Family* and its adaptation for the stage and screen as *All the Way Home*. The play was the basis for an opera.

Signs and portents are to be found in all of them, the ever-present thanatopsis intensifying with Agee's approaching death at the age of forty-five. On November 16, 1952, the first of his four-part treatment of Lincoln, "Abraham Lincoln—The Early Years," appeared on "Omnibus," a television series produced by Robert Saudek, his college roommate. On that crisp autumn evening, Agee's words were heard by millions of viewers, who witnessed a birth and a prophecy, as from the perspective of the stars:

> One hard night in February in 1809, they looked down on a little cabin in a fold of the Kentucky hills; and they saw how it all began: a very humble and obscure event; as ordinary as death. But not even the stars in their elderly wisdom could dream what was to rise up out of this beginning.[80]

A few days after Agee's death on May 16, 1955, Father James Flye, his former teacher and close friend, found on the writer's mantle in his New York apartment a letter addressed to him in an airmail envelope. In the letter Agee discussed an idea for a film script he intended to write. A herd of African elephants converge toward the disembodied voice of God, who confesses He has given up his omnipotence "when I gave to Man the Will to love me or to hate me, or merely to disregard me. So I can promise you nothing." He warns the elephants that a new age has begun, an age in which they will not only be captured and used for work, but exhibited and ridiculed.

> As I said, I am not omnipotent; I can't even prophesy: I ask only this: be your good selves, always faithfully, always in knowledge of my love and regard, and through so being, you may convert those heathen, those barbarians, where all else has failed.

At the end of the story, thirty-six elephants die in a fire. "Their huge souls, light as clouds, settle like doves, in the great secret cemetery back in Africa—And perhaps God speaks, tenderly, again; perhaps saying: 'The Peace of God, which passeth all understanding. . . .'"[81]

He had heard those final words, written by St. Paul, many times in the liturgy of *The Book of Common Prayer*, and they could serve with the story as Agee's final prophecy for the human race. God Himself, he seemed to suggest, could not know the future, but He could share in human suffering and offer the saving balm of divine love. God had spoken; the rest was up to mankind.

And mankind could find in this world no clearer mirror of its condition than the figure the child Rufus had seen on the movie screen with his father: Chaplin's Tramp, "the most humane and most nearly complete among the religious figures of our time."[82] In a 1949 article for *Life* magazine, Agee comments on the conclusion of Chaplin's *City Lights*, in which the Tramp causes a blind girl to regain her sight. "She has imagined and anticipated him as princely, to say the least; and it has never seriously occurred to him that he is inadequate," he writes. "She recognizes who he must be by his shy, confident, shining joy as he comes silently toward her. And he recognizes himself, for the first time, through the terrible changes in her face. The camera just exchanges a few quiet close-ups of the emotions which shift and intensify in each face. It is enough to shrivel the heart to see," he says, "and it is the greatest piece of acting and the highest moment in movies."[83]

Like the Tramp he loved, James Agee the Seer tried to give sight to the blind and found in their eyes, if only for a supernal moment, the reflection of his own shining joy.

## Notes

1.  *James Agee: Selected Journalism*, ed. Paul Ashdown (Knoxville: U of Tennessee P, 1985), 161.
2.  T. S. Matthews, *Angels Unawares* (New York: Ticknor & Fields, 1985), 161.
3.  *James Agee: Selected Journalism*, ed. Ashdown, 161.
4.  George P. Landow, *Elegant Jeremiahs* (Ithaca: Cornell UP, 1986), 17–40. Professor W. H. Greenleaf of University College, Swansea, noticed similarities between Agee and Carlyle and kindly suggested them to me. For

background on Carlyle and his times, see Greenleaf's *The British Political Tradition*, 2 vols. (New York: Methuen, 1983).

5. Landow, *Elegant Jeremiahs*, 191.

6. William Stott's classic study *Documentary Expression and Thirties America* (Chicago: U of Chicago P, 1986) offers invaluable perspective. It would be interesting to consider in some detail the similarities and differences between documentary reporting, as Stott has defined it, and contemporary prophetic nonfiction writing. Other standard works include *The New Journalism*, ed. Tom Wolfe and E. W. Johnson (New York: Harper, 1973); Shelley Fisher Fishkin, *From Fact to Fiction* (Baltimore: Johns Hopkins UP, 1985); *The Literary Journalists*, ed. Norman Sims (New York: Ballantine, 1984); and Ronald Weber, *The Literature of Fact: Literary Nonfiction in American Writing* (Athens: Ohio UP, 1980).

7. *Collected Short Prose of James Agee*, ed. Robert Fitzgerald (New York: Ballantine, 1970), 160.

8. Ibid., 148.

9. James Agee, *Permit Me Voyage* (New Haven: Yale UP, 1934).

10. "A Memoir by Robert Fitzgerald," in *Collected Short Prose of James Agee*, ed. Fitzgerald, 26–27.

11. Alfred T. Barson, *A Way of Seeing* (Amherst: U of Massachusetts P, 1972), 54–55.

12. James Agee, "Good Friday," *The Harvard Advocate Anniversary Anthology*, ed. Douglas A. McIntyre and Karen S. Hull (Cambridge: Schenkman, 1987), 134.

13. Sir James George Frazer, *The Golden Bough* (New York: Macmillan, 1951), 184.

14. Thomas Bulfinch, *The Age of Fable* (New York: Heritage, 1942), 170–72, 298–99.

15. Thomas Carlyle, *The Life of John Sterling*, 2d ed. (Boston: Phillips, Sampson, 1852), 74.

16. James Agee, *A Death in the Family* (New York: McDowell, Obolensky, 1957), 80–84.

17. Ibid., 3–22.

18. Richard N. Owen, Sr., *Recollections and Reassurances* (Nashville, TN: privately published, 1982); telephone interview, 23 Jan. 1988.

19. Advertising circular for Fountain Place Condominiums.

20. Agee to John Huston, 14 Sept. 1950, John Huston Papers, Margaret Herrick Library, Academy of Motion Picture Arts and Sciences, Los Angeles, CA, qtd. Laurence Bergreen, *James Agee: A Life* (New York: Dutton, 1984), 29.

21. Edward Blair Bolles, "Exeter in the Ordovician," *Exeter Remembered*, ed. Henry Darcy Curwen (Exeter, NH: Phillips Exeter Academy, 1965), 137.

22. James Agee and Walker Evans, *Let Us Now Praise Famous Men* (Boston: Houghton, 1960), 374.

23. *Letters of James Agee to Father Flye*, 2d ed. (Dunwoody, GA: Norman S. Berg, 1978), 56.

24. Ibid., 58.
25. Roy Hoopes, *Ralph Ingersoll* (New York: Atheneum, 1985), 86–88.
26. *Letters of James Agee to Father Flye*, 68; Geneviève Moreau, *The Restless Journey of James Agee* (New York: Morrow, 1977), 119–20.
27. Hoopes, *Ralph Ingersoll*, 86.
28. *James Agee: Selected Journalism*, ed. Ashdown, 30, 29, 9, 130.
29. Hoopes, *Ralph Ingersoll*, 99.
30. Karal Ann Marling, *The Colossus of Roads* (Minneapolis: U of Minnesota P, 1984), 42–43.
31. Bergreen, *James Agee: A Life*, 65–71.
32. Donald Martin Reynolds, *The Architecture of New York* (New York: Macmillan, 1984), 238; May C. Callas and Wallace H. Randolph, *Inside 42nd Street*, program booklet for exhibition sponsored by Historical Buildings Committee of New York Chapter of American Institute of Architects, 1978; Paul Fussell, *Abroad* (New York: Oxford UP, 1980), 50–51.
33. *Collected Short Prose of James Agee*, ed. Fitzgerald, 3; James J. Flink, *The Automobile Age* (Cambridge, MA: MIT Press, 1988), 207; Vic Weals, "Remembering the Wreck That Made a Writer," *Knoxville Journal*, 23 Apr. 1986.
34. *James Agee: Selected Journalism*, ed. Ashdown, 43.
35. Flink, *The Automobile Age*, 188–228.
36. Frederick Lewis Allen, *The Big Change* (New York: Harper, 1952), 129.
37. *James Agee: Selected Journalism*, ed. Ashdown, 42.
38. Hoopes, *Ralph Ingersoll*, 99–100.
39. *James Agee: Selected Journalism*, ed. Ashdown, 42–62.
40. Warren James Belasco, *Americans on the Road* (Cambridge: MIT Press, 1979), 145.
41. *Letters of James Agee to Father Flye*, 87.
42. George Walker, *Saratoga* (Englewood Cliffs, NJ: Prentice-Hall, 1966), 325, 312, 337–38.
43. *James Agee: Selected Journalism*, ed. Ashdown, 113.
44. Walker, *Saratoga*, 334.
45. *Collected Short Prose of James Agee*, ed. Fitzgerald, 5.
46. Agee and Evans, *Let Us Now Praise Famous Men*, 5.
47. Jane Gibbs DuBose, "Whittle's 'Campus' Unveiled," *Knoxville News-Sentinel*, 2 Oct. 1986.
48. Agee and Evans, *Let Us Now Praise Famous Men*, 405.
49. Ibid., 249.
50. Ibid., 51.
51. Ibid., 415.
52. Ibid., 35.
53. Ibid., 249.
54. *Agee on Film: Reviews and Comments* (Boston: Beacon, 1964), 143.
55. Stott, *Documentary Expression and Thirties America*, 313.
56. Ibid., 311–12.
57. Dale Maharidge and Michael Williamson, *And Their Children After Them* (New York: Pantheon, 1989), 208.

58. W. H. Auden, 16 Oct. 1944. The letter appears in *Agee on Film.*
59. *Agee on Film,* 104.
60. Ibid., 60.
61. Ibid., 152.
62. Ibid., 159–60.
63. Ibid., 55.
64. Ibid., 125.
65. Ibid., 243.
66. Ibid., 278.
67. Ibid., 136, 65.
68. Ibid., 168.
69. Ibid., 181.
70. Ibid., 80.
71. Ibid., 203.
72. Ibid., 224.
73. Ibid., 275.
74. Ibid., 148.
75. Ibid., 285.
76. Ibid., 286.
77. Ibid., 286.
78. Ibid., 287.
79. Ibid., 278.
80. "Abraham Lincoln—The Early Years," in *The Lively Arts: Four Representative Types,* ed. Rodney E. Sheratsky and John L. Reilly (New York: Globe, 1964), 385.
81. *Letters of James Agee to Father Flye,* 228–32.
82. *Agee on Film,* 262.
83. Ibid., 10.

# Mood and Music:
# Landscape and Artistry in
# *A Death in the Family*

*Eugene T. Carroll*

A DEATH IN THE FAMILY is a unique, undemanding, and personal novel, devoid of either a gripping plot, diverse settings, a multitude of unforgettable characters, or a plethora of action-filled chapters. Instead, the plot is simple and muted; the setting is quiet Knoxville at the beginning of the twentieth century; the characters are ordinary and unblemished in their innocence; and the chapters ebb and flow on the tides of life, love, home, family, death, and resurrection.

What make this novel universally appealing is its unusual ability to generate a finely tuned set of perceptions for reader and critic alike. Agee, with his exquisite use of the "precise" word in the metrical sensibilities of poetic and musical prose, has taken an ordinary event and transformed it onto an extraordinary stage of understanding and solemnity without stiff or rigid boundaries. Almost Wagnerian at times in its soaring and lyrical beauty, the novel, like its author, is restless, moving from image to image, from life to death to resurrection, from shades of black to gray to white, and from character to character against the backdrop of Agee's own childhood and the death of his father. Richard Hayes, writing of Agee's ability to circumvent human time, without falling into the abyss of dullness, notes that he gives very little articulation to plot and focuses instead on death and grief in a dramatic mode: "What it takes of substance after the single incident is a dramatized ritual of those moments—

hours and days, weeks perhaps, even longer—in which we do not live but merely endure."[1] Kenneth Seib echoes Hayes by contending that *A Death in the Family* touches upon no social or psychological problems of the 1950s but rather is a simple story told as "a tightly constructed work . . . with the dramatized structure and tensions of a play and the lyrical intensity of a poem."[2] The story is played out on a human stage with a "sense of childhood, family protection and small-town revery that is uniquely American."[3]

Agee, in the first two decades after his death in 1955, was viewed more as a cult figure than as a major writer, partly because of the small canon of his writing and the social and literary milieu of those years, but probably more so because his critics were either friends (Robert Fitzgerald, David McDowell, and Father James Flye) whose remembrances were often, as Mark Doty notes, "colored largely by intimate association with him,"[4] or critic-friends (Wilbur Frohock and Dwight Macdonald) who thought he destroyed his artistic potential through his disparaging life-style, or literary writer-critics (Peter Ohlin and Kenneth Seib) who ignored his excesses and concentrated exclusively on his art. Almost entirely autobiographical in his canon of writing, Agee sees his vision and his world through wide-ranging lenses to include all written genres. In the preface to *The Letters of James Agee to Father Flye*, for example, Robert Phelps, a close friend, notes that, even in an often-neglected area such as personal correspondence, Agee "inhabited" his letters: "In every one of these letters a human being is present: not just his beliefs and notions and moods, but something containing all these elements, that elusive essence of a complex personality which it takes a good novelist to purvey."[5] On the other hand, Frohock, in his *The Novel of Violence* in America, argues that, while Agee in *A Death in the Family* demonstrated that he had the literary techniques and abilities to become a major novelist, his "accomplishments are quickly listed and seem only mildly impressive."[6] Macdonald, as well, in *Against the American Grain*, insists that Agee could have written major works that would have made him a major writer immediately, but because he insisted on working on a wider range of writing interests and assignments, his "was a wasted and wasteful life."[7]

However, despite the varied opinions of unique and friendly or unfriendly critics, the Agee legend has shifted dramatically from the controversies surrounding his life versus his art to a recognition of his unusual and skillful perception of very common people and his ability to elevate them, through his cinematic eye and musical ear, to a newer and more abstract but unified vision of himself, his fellow man, all of creation, and his God. *A Death in the Family* is a religious book, deeply rooted in southern faith, conversion, salvation, and tradition, never maudlin and never overbearing. The unified vision of his own life as a child and the tragic loss of his youthful father gave Agee the opportunity to draw deeply into his own introspection, a major key to his own religious experiences, and to empathize strongly with the novel's characters, even to a mild and inoffensive way, with Ralph and Father Jackson. Agee, in essence, is not simply a poet, novelist, film critic, screenplay writer, and short-story author separately, but rather he acts as a catalyst, adapter, an overseer, so to speak, of all he surveys. He is always the "writer" above anything else, a writer-artist, whose poetic and language-filled canvases, in many cases, are uniquely southern, and focus, not only on the rural landscape of the South, and particularly Tennessee, but on the universality of those eternal values of place, time, family, and remembrance.

The newer critics, indeed, recognizing Agee's ubiquity, see his work as rich, refreshing, visionary, and many-leveled; J. A. Ward uses *A Death in the Family* as a measure of how silence dominates its country landscape and how the lack of flowing dialogue propels its themes and plot.[8] Rufus, Jay, Mary, Hannah, Ralph, and Andrew, among others, are ethereal characters drawn from the past and set against a "blue dew" background; they demonstrate images of another day and time in which living and life were slower, more gracious, and more meaningful. Robert Coles, a noted Agee enthusiast, in his *Irony in the Mind's Eye* likewise employs *A Death in the Family* to illustrate the role of childhood in the life of Rufus (Agee) as a part of remembrance of what Knoxville was like in the 1900s with the experiences of life, death, and resurrection—the triune themes of the novel—so closely interwoven. With death as one constant theme, Coles writes that despite such an emphasis "Agee unquestionably has a consistent vision of the child's special kind of human situation, and he wants to unfold the vision before us unobtrusively but as fully as the Follet family and their fortunes (or moment of awful misfortune) will permit him."[9]

William John Rewak, in his 1970 dissertation on Agee, sees *A Death in the Family* as a simple novel that reaffirms middle-class values, the small town in the rural South, and the lives of very special people. Like most of the modern critics, including Ward and Coles, Rewak finds that the novel provides Agee with an opportunity to draw on his past, through the eyes of Rufus, "to discover a meaning for the present."[10] The emphasis, then, is not so much on a death, Rewak asserts, but on the "response of maturation that results from a confrontation with death."[11]

By 1989, the eightieth anniversary of Agee's birth, *A Death in the Family* had become a standard work, a mainstream novel, for serious and eclectic readers who strive to synthesize their artistic and literary interests. Essentially, the setting of Knoxville and the atmosphere of the simple life combine to create visionary and artistic qualities in Agee's conception of home, family, love, death, resurrection, and, especially, faith. The Follet family passes through a period of "standing time," focusing only on the death of the young husband and father, Jay, and then move through their individual moods of grief and loss to those of acceptance and resurrection. Agee's orchestration of the patterns of life and death for each family member creates poetic and musical fusion and produces a symphonic blend of interwoven emotional movements.

The setting of Knoxville, for example, signals Agee's ever-present and continued search for family roots, place, meaning, and selfhood. This Tennessee town and its rural environment serve as backdrops for at least two poems by Agee, one entitled "Sunday: Outskirts of Knoxville, Tenn.,"[12] the other, "Knoxville: Summer of 1915," the latter first appearing in a 1938 issue of *Partisan Review*[13] and later as the prologue to *A Death in the Family* as compiled and edited by David McDowell.[14] The two poems are different in several basic ways: first, the former deals specifically with the theme of youthful love and what results as that kind of love is diminished and broken. Peter Ohlin, writing of Agee's poetic gifts, and particularly of "Sunday: Outskirts of Knoxville, Tenn.," notes: "Its tone, for instance, moves from the idyll to a somber meditation to a furious vision and concludes with compassionate prayer."[15] Elizabeth Drew, praising Agee for his tenderness and sympathy in the poem, keenly observes how he "supports his outer and inner landscapes with an interweaving of skillful verbal patterns."[16] Second, "Knoxville: Summer of 1915" is more autobiographical and relates more specifically to the Agee family. A vivid and sensual presentation of Agee's own life as a child, the poem is a creative and musical experience, a striking example of the poet "inside the word," fusing "remembrance" with the present. Macdonald calls "Knoxville: Summer of 1915" typical of Agee's work because of the "weighty authority with which words are selected and placed."[17]

Agee, in "Knoxville," recaptures his own vision of his childhood and his early years, centering primarily on the simple landscapes of the ordinary life of the rural South; with the whole family as reference, he sets the tone and the mood of the book as well as the atmosphere of the coming life-death-life rituals. The poem's words are "precise" in meaning and mood, painting a delicate but complete picture of the variations in life's frailties. Rufus, as soloist, here and in the other interpolated prose-poems, affirms the counter-theme of life, though, as Jeanne Concannon points out, "against the omnipresent and inevitable themes of death, doubt, fear, confusion and loneliness."[18]

Charles Mayo, in his 1969 dissertation, notes in some detail that "Knoxville" was used by the American composer Samuel Barber in 1947 as a text on which to base a work for the American soprano Eleanor Steber. Agee, incidentally, was prevented from attending the premiere of this work in Boston because of hospitalization, an ironic twist of fate, considering his love and use of music within all of his work. The composition was referred to, according to critic David Johnson in his notes for the recording, quoted in Mayo's work, as "a small miracle; technically a miracle because asymmetrical prose has been given complete musical symmetry; and an expressive miracle because it fuses poet, musician, singer and listener into one celebrant of the American experience."[19] The musical sounds of the poem's words in the Barber composition parallel a sense of childhood, a need for love and protection, and a reverence for the landscapes of "place" and generation. Barber's composition has a simple tone-poem quality. Its opening lines, "Knoxville . . . it has become that time of evening when people sit on their porches, rocking gently and talking gently and watching the street . . ." (6), confront, first, a day's-end ritual

It has be-come that time of eve - ning when peo-ple

sit on their por - ches, rock - ing gent-ly and talk - ing gent - ly

and watch-ing the street

From Samuel Barber, Knoxville: *Summer of 1915* (New York: Schirmer, 1952).
Used by permission of the publisher.

that has been continuous through generations, a reflective period after the day's work, and second, the reaffirmation of "place" in family
life. But even more so, it details intimately what it feels like to sit on a
porch in the evening, to listen to the "nozzle" watering the lawn and
to hear the "crickets" and the "locusts."

"Knoxville," musically and naturally, divides into five parts with
the main theme (see figure) of eight measures; it moves at a leisurely
pace with the blending of soft strings and predominant woodwinds
to present the effect of a still and undistractible evening. Only once,
in the first part, is that pace interrupted, as the orchestra simulates
for undistinguished seconds the sound of a "loud" automobile. In the
second part, the streetcar is heard for the first time, loud, agitated,
hurried and "belling," a symbolic image that will be repeated again
and again throughout the novel proper; the streetcar is the symbol
and vehicle moving the minimal plot and raising aloft to three-di-
mensional force the triune themes of life, death, and resurrection.
In the third part, Barber combines some of Agee's most sensuous
images into measures of color and sound to focus on the strongest
kinds of "remembrance" and "memorial." In visually exquisite
phrases, capable of standing alone or locked into time, mood, and
music, the language of "Knoxville" goes beyond the actual meaning
of the American experience, that simplicity of small-town living, and

brings a universality to life and death. The sounds and phrases of "blue dew" or "a frailing of fire" or "from damp strings morning glories—hang their ancient faces" (7) are reminiscent in their poetic forms and harmonies of some of Agee's literary heroes and mentors, Walt Whitman, Stephen Crane, Hart Crane, and Emily Dickinson. Barber encloses these phrases in harmonic measures of expressive pictures; he captures the form of the work in movement and space.

In the fourth part, a variation of the first theme is heard as the "remembered" family spreads "quilts" on the wet grass in the backyard, comfortable and close to each other: "We all lie there, my mother, my father, my uncle, my aunt, and I too am lying there" (7), talking very little and of nothing in particular. Agee's "stop-camera" effect within a musical form and Barber's tonal picture of "The stars are wide and alive, they seem each like a smile of great sweetness and they seem very near" (7) unite in a unique application of the inner and outer landscapes of truth and beauty. Even the momentarily rich but dissonant sounds of "By some chance, here they are, all on this earth . . ." (8) and the strong, surging quality of the prayer, "May God bless my people, my uncle, my aunt, my mother, my good father . . ."(8), raise the solemnity of the tone poem to a supernatural level with spiritual and religious overtones. Finally, part five, a codetta, or, a small coda ". . . but will not, oh, will not, not now, not ever, but will not ever tell me who I am . . ." (8) reinforces the "remembrance" of childhood, of father-loss, the lifelong search for selfhood and the universality of man and his God.

If "Knoxville" reveals Agee's special visual and poetic gifts, his techniques of "flowing musical language" bring to the critical reader's immediate consciousness both the Wordsworthian concept that the poet acts, feels, thinks, and writes in the spirit of human passions and emotions[20] and the Wagnerian resolution of continuous music or "endless melody." Agee succeeds in extending or crystallizing the rich and emotional event of a family death with compassion and feeling, interweaving those emotions with the homespun values of joy, love, sorrow, and intimate concern. *A Death in the Family* is clearly and significantly alive with direct or indirect music or musical imagery. In at least a half-dozen encounters with other members of the family, Agee, through Rufus, interlaces music and mood to conceptualize the unity of plot, setting, characters, and themes, and, through the "stream of time," brings coherence and cohesion to the novel's unusual framework, elements all calculated to move from Jay's death to the family's grieving period and finally to the resurrection of Jay's spirit in the butterfly sequence.

In his early Harvard years, Agee, in a long, thoughtful, and well-known letter to Father Flye, contends that, beside his poetic skill, he longs to compose music and to direct movies that he has authored. A little later he writes of his empathy with people, his need to combine their dramas and to bring together their emotions: "the whole—words, emotions, characters, situation, etc.—has a discernible symmetry and a very definite musical quality—inaccurately speaking—I want to write symphonies. That is, characters introduced quietly (as are themes in a symphony, say) will recur in new lights, with new verbal orchestration, will work into counterpoint and get a sort of monstrous grinding beauty—and so on."[21]

*A Death in the Family,* by and large, demonstrates Agee's strong and gifted sense of symphonic form, not only in the poetic and imagistic movements of each of the parts but in the interplay between sets of characters who, as Concannon points out, "move together and apart in a dance-like rhythm of dialogue and introspection."[22] In Part 1, Rufus is not always sure of his father in their duet of men's night out, i.e., the Chaplin film, the bar scene (where there is no music), and the nightscape of Knoxville. Agee's landscape at night details in duet the innocence of memory, Rufus in concert with his father, every sound recorded: "Deep in the valley an engine coughed and browsed; couplings settled their long chains, and the empty cars sounded like broken drums" (18) or "Sometimes on these evenings his father would hum a little and the humming would break open into a word or two, but he never finished a part of a tune, for silence was even more pleasurable. . . ." (20). The warm dark night is interrupted only twice for quick glimpses of Agee's perennial memory, momentary flashes of "the odd, shaky light of Market Square" (15), and incongruity of life and picture: "A dark-faced man leaned against the white brick wall, gnawing a turnip; he looked at them with sad, pale eyes, . . . and Rufus, turning, saw how he looked sorrowfully, somewhat dangerously, after them"(15). A moment later, Jay and Rufus pass a wagon with a large sleeping family and a woman wearing a sunbonnet: "Rufus's father averted his eyes and touched his straw hat slightly; and Rufus, looking back, saw how her dead eyes kept looking gently ahead of her" (15). Even later, the father and the son, the duet of love and contentment, sit on a rock above North Knoxville: "There were no words, or even ideas, or formed emotions, of the kind that have been suggested here, no more in the man than in the boy child" (20). Agee builds image upon image of "dark night," interlocking the time frames of his father's last evening of life and Rufus's own feelings of security and trust despite the sadness of the "dark-faced" man and the "dead eyes" of the woman near the wagon. The first chapter ends, Rewak points out, as the father and the son walk in silence, "the rest of the way home" (22), and the last chapter will end as Rufus and Andrew walk "all the way home" (339). "Between these two events," Rewak concludes, "Agee has built around the word, 'home,' the connotations of peace and strength but also death and fear."[23]

In the second chapter of Part 1, Agee shifts, with poetic and musical skill, to the relationship between husband and wife, Jay and Mary, as the former prepares to leave in the middle of the night to visit his ailing father. Their "domestic particulars" are both comedic and serious; Mary is prudish and overly religious while Jay, not always successful in the "verities" of home and family, tries to remember what to do outwardly, "Bring your *shoes*—to the kitchen" (29), and inwardly, so as not to awaken the children. Mary, the wife and mother, the epitome of domesticity, symbolizes a part of the Follet family's strong belief in warmth and strength. Jay prepares to leave the bedroom when he turns to look at the unmade bed: "Well, he thought, I can do something for her. . . . He drew the covers up to keep the warmth, then laid them open a few inches, so it would look inviting to get into" (31). His movement is nostalgic, remembering sensitive and husbandly details: things, little things that mean so much. Mary's breakfast for Jay is large today: eggs, bacon, pancakes, and coffee. Jay returns the favor by heating warm milk, an image to be repeated in later chapters: "She poured the white, softly steaming milk into a thick, white cup and sat down with it. . . . Because of the strangeness of the hour and the abrupt destruction of sleep, the necessity for action and its interruptive minutiae, the gravity of his errand and a kind of weary exhilaration, both of them found it peculiarly hard to talk, though both particularly wanted to" (34). Now as Jay prepares to leave, Mary "remembers" a new clean pocket handkerchief; the couple walks to the edge of the porch, where "deep in the end of the back yard, the blossoming peach tree shone like a celestial sentinel" (38), and they struggle with departure in their goodbyes. Even the customary morning rhyme is "remembered" but not sung: "Goodby, John, don't stay long / I'll be back in a week or two" (39).

Agee, in the next several chapters, enlarges on the fundamental character and personalities of Jay, Ralph (his brother), and Mary as they react to their own particularly interior landscapes, a blending of picture and tone. Jay drives from the warmth of his hearth to the black unknown ahead of him as he leaves Knoxville behind: "Along his right were dark vacant lots, pale billboards, the darker blocks of small sleeping buildings, an occasional light" (43), to "that kind of flea-bitten rurality" (43) with "mean little homes . . . mean little pieces of ill-cultivated land behind them" (44), and a "late, late streetcar, no passengers aboard, far out near the end of its run" (44). After his encounter with the ferryman, who, like Charon, gives him a final ride across the river, he finds that the land becomes more familiar, "real, old, deep country now. Home country" (48). The simplicity of life, the landscape of "place" is here at home, "where he felt much more deeply at leisure as he watched the flowing, freshly lighted country; and quite consciously he drove a little faster than before" (48).

Mary's landscape, on the other hand, is one of guilt or religiosity, symbolized by the "white" sleep. Her concern centers not so much on her husband's leaving but on her unspoken and sometimes unconscious feelings about her father-in-law because "everyone forgave him so much and liked him so well in spite of his shortcomings . . . a kind of weakness which took advantage and heaped disadvantage and burden on others" (50–51). If the call in the night concerned her mother-in-law, Mary would have felt differently. She turns to prayer, when "I almost *wished* for his death!" (52), and she immediately reverts to her religious scruples, praying for help and understanding for herself, her father-in-law, and her husband. Her landscape, unsettled at times, is peopled, though, with the intimate and loving associates of family, Jay, Rufus, her daughter Catherine, and Aunt Hannah: "I must just: trust in God. . . . Just do His will, and put all my trust in Him" (54). The "stream of whiteness" breaks as she awakens to another day: "A streetcar passed: Catherine cried" (54).

Ralph's landscape is one of self-pity and the bottle, and while Agee paints a dismal picture of a man incapable of giving or even feeling love, he never condemns him, only letting the color and odor of irresponsibility, self-destruction and helplessness strongly stand out. When Ralph approached his mother to show his affection for her, she turned away, knowing that "he was beseeching comfort rather than bringing it" (62). Agee's Ralph is a pathetic character, reeking of booze and self-pity, a slobbering figure of a man, fat, disgusting, and uninteresting to all, including his wife. A one-dimensional human, Ralph contrasts sharply with Jay and almost any other man in his narrow frame of reference; even the house hand, Tom Oaks, can ask the mother if he is needed and to call if she wants anything. Ralph's shame borders on self-hatred, and his landscape, like a wild, erratic storm, defeats him constantly. When one of life's strongest and most inevitable tests come to his family, "one of the times in a man's life when he is needed and can be some good, just by being a man" (70), Ralph fails and ends up as a weakling.

In the fifth, sixth, and seventh chapters of Part 1, Agee begins to escalate the whole thematic structure of the novel into small, delicate, comedic or serious moments, exquisite scenes of "standing time." Moods become like movements of a symphonic piece—some slow, some fast, some moderate in tone with flowing, endless themes and counter-themes. Some of the scenes bring the human spirit back into focus; others show grim turns of grief and loss, and still others extend more understanding and peace. In the fifth chapter, for example, Rufus, when told by his mother of the possibility that his grandfather might die, comes to grips, momentarily, with what a loss is all about and equates the possible passing of his grandfather with the death of his cat: "Mama," Rufus said, "when Oliver went to sleep, did he wake up in heaven too" (56)? Mary, startled but always straitlaced, and always relying on what the church teaches about death, fends Rufus off with meaningless adult answers that center, first, upon the anxiety that the children should finish breakfast and prepare for school, and second, with the repetitious "I don't know." Within the purest realm of childlike reasoning, Rufus satisfied himself about who gets into heaven in the case of the rabbits who were bloodied to death by the dogs: "Why did God let the dogs in" (56)? Mary, agitated but resigned, replies, "We mustn't trouble ourselves with these things we can't understand. We just have to be sure that God knows best" (56). Rufus plays the comedic and unexpected role: "I bet they sneaked in when He wasn't looking. . . . Cause He sure wouldn't have let them in if He'd been there. Didn't they Mama? Didn't they" (57)? Mary once again retreats to the church's stand, this time speaking theologically of good or evil and God or the devil, playing a rapid-fire but unwieldy exchange with Rufus, whose only repeated words are "what" or "why." She opens with the word "tempts"; he seizes onto that word and asks: "What's tempt?" She hesitates and says: "the Devil tempts us when there is something we want to do, but we know it is bad." Rufus continues the momentum: "Why does God let us do bad things?" Mary: "Because He wants us to make up our own minds." "Why" is the continually drumming word for Rufus, but finally the dialogue ends with Mary's carefully spaced words, which are intended to be emphatic: "God—doesn't—believe—in—the—easy—way." Catherine, innocent and wide-eyed through the exchange, injects another comedic touch: "Like hide-and-go-seek" (57). Rufus, agitated and angry, blusters at her: "God doesn't fool around playing games, does He, Mama! Does He! Does He!" Rufus, unbowed by his mother's defense of his sister but aware that he must apologize for unbecoming behavior, says unwittingly: "I *am* sorry, Catherine. . . . Honest to goodness I am. Because you're a little, *little* girl . . . " (59). Not realizing what he had just said and how it affected Catherine, Rufus is sent "brusquely" off to school.

Agee's women, like Mary and little Catherine, symbolize a sense of gentility, the love and respect for home and "place," but more than any other characteristic, they instinctively and successfully balance the need for the virtues of faith, hope, love, and even reserve, to be alive and vibrant. Mary, for example, is patient and giving, and unlike Jay, she demonstrates an interior of self-restraint. Those attributes become more apparent in another scene, when Rufus (Agee) accepts an invitation to go shopping with Mary's Aunt Hannah, whom Rewak calls "the strongest character in the book."[24] Mary and Hannah are much alike, at this point, and although the aunt is older and wiser, her feelings toward her niece are from a completely interior point of view and never spoken. When Hannah asks Mary if Rufus would like to go shopping with her, Mary's tone in return is reserved and hesitant. Hannah is "tempted to tell her not to make up children's minds for them but held onto herself . . ." (71).

In the afternoon, when the two leave for the shopping tour, the streetcar carries them to Gay Street and the stores. Once inside, Rufus pays little attention to what his great-aunt is doing or saying; he focuses instead on "the clashing, banging wire baskets which hastened along on little trolleys, high above them all, bearing to and fro wrapped and unwrapped merchandise, and hard leather cylinders full of money" (75). The contrast between the two sharpens vividly when Hannah asks Rufus if he would like a new cap; as they move to men's furnishings, Hannah's eyes fall on "a genteel dark serge with the all but invisible visor, which she was sure would please Mary, . . . " but Rufus's senses were "set on a thunderous fleecy check in jade green, canary yellow, black and white, which stuck out inches to either side above his ears and had a great scoop of visor beneath which his face was all but lost" (78). Aunt Hannah thinks of the reaction from Mary, perhaps even Jay, and certainly the boys on the block, but she refrains from comment; Rufus likes the cap and she buys it. Agee's treatment of Aunt Hannah is one of respect for age, wisdom, and strength of character. She personifies a two-tiered dimension of womanhood: first, in elegance, graciousness, beauty, and a love of "remembrance," and second, in the awareness of the youth and vigor of the generations behind her. Agee's keen wit about Hannah is apparent with a reference to her "pouring gravely through an issue of 'The Nation'" (73).

As theme and counter-theme, life and death move slowly or rapidly through the sensibilities of these characters or their responses to their day and to each other. The interpolated prose-poems after chapter 7 support a different tonality, the overwhelming memories of Rufus as a child with loving parents nearby. Ohlin, writing of these memories, argues: "The long lyrical section describing Rufus's fear of the dark (80–85) goes so far beyond anything that could possibly be characterized as the child's awareness that it becomes, in effect, expressive of Agee's effort to move inside the experience rather than of the experience itself."[25] Rufus fears the blackness and the premonition of the death that will shortly take place; in this nightmare of time, unlike the peace and tranquility of "Knoxville," Rufus, as an infant in a crib, can see and hear "a serpent shape" on the wallpaper or voices like locusts that "cared nothing for him" before Jay came in to quiet him. Rufus "remembers" Jackie, the cloth dog, and remembers his father singing familiar songs, some old, some popular: "Frog he would a wooin' go un-hooooo," "I got a gallon on a sugarbabe too," or "Google Eyes," and the old and loving spiritual, "Git on board, little children" (93). Mary also sang softer and more maternal songs to Rufus, perhaps because she was pregnant with Catherine. He liked "Sleep, baby sleep," "Go tell Aunt Rhoda," but especially, "Swing low, sweet cherryut," sung either by his father or mother; the reflection is on home, the meaning of home, the journey of life to death, and is summed up in "Comin' for to care me home" (98). Agee's mood and tone, like that of Thomas Wolfe, his sonorities of sound in music, of distance and nearness, of simplicity and complexity, reverberate in: "How far we all come. How far we all come away from ourselves. . . . you can never go home again. You can go home, it's good to go home, but you never really get all the way home again in your life" (94).

Agee's sensitive perceptions of his father reflect the strongest kinds of images of Jay (100–101), with detailed precision of what he wore—for example, "hard" pants, "hard" coats, "hard" celluloid collars, and "hard" buttons on a vest; or of the smells associated with maleness—i.e., "dry grass, leather and tobacco"; or of the case of a big mustache, not particularly enjoyed by Mary. When Jay was talking about the "mush'tash," "he was joking, talking like a darky. He liked to talk darky talk and the way he sang was like a darky too, only when he sang he wasn't joking" (101). Rufus, too, becomes reacquainted with a "darky" or "colored" in a scene with Victoria, black Victoria, who had taken care of him when he was born; now that Mary is about to give birth to Catherine, she reemerges to take him to his "Granma's." Mary cautions Rufus not to refer to her color or her "smell"; Rufus, throwing caution to the wind, asks directly: "Why is your skin so dark," and Victoria answers: "Just because that was the way God made me" (109). Against the background of a "yellow streetcar," Victoria reminds Rufus that he should be more careful about asking a "colored" why her skin is dark, but adds lovingly: "You make me feel happy. . . . I missed you terribly, honey" (110). Agee's finely tuned senses, like the mechanics of the streetcar, move the experiential memories beyond the darkness and the light and signal life as is was in another time and death as it is to be.

In Part 2, the daily lives of Mary, Andrew (her brother), and Aunt Hannah, in particular, and others in general, come to an abrupt halt as Jay's death becomes a part of their sensibilities. Mary sends her brother to find out if Jay is injured or dead, and in the meantime she prepares the downstairs bedroom for what may be a long convalescence, brings "clean sheets and pillowcases" to the bed, plumping and smoothing the pillows, bringing out the bedpan and the thermometer, replacing the guest towels, every action designed to relieve the tension, and finally, falling down on her knees, to utter the words of the Cross she knows so well: "O God if it be Thy will." With Hannah at her side, Mary begins her long vigil of faith and hope, small talk, and tea as the symbol of warmth. Time, as a measure of day and night, disappears; conversation becomes inactive, and silence pervades as the two women wait and wait and wait. "Mary did not speak, and Hannah could not think of a word to say. It was absurd, she realized, but along with everything else, she felt almost of a kind of social embarrassment about her speechlessness" (131). Hannah, thirty years ago, lost and grieved as Mary would tonight. The women pray an alternate litany for God's forgiveness and quietly say the "Our Father." The rhythms of life have closed down, and with every tick of the clock and Andrew's absence or lack of a phone call, death is no longer a possibility but a truth.

Finally, after long hours of waiting, Andrew brings the fatal news to the waiting women, and Mary, alone now as a widow, says in a small voice: "I want whiskey," to preserve a closeness, a last bond with Jay: "I want it just as strong as I can stand it" (149). Andrew, in concert with Mary, plays his double role as loving brother and uneasy messenger with honesty and devotion. The other members quickly come to the house, Mary's father offering philosophical words for her sorrow and loss: "Just spunk won't be enough; you've got to have gumption" (155). The family hears details of the accident and death for their needs and knowledge. Andrew—as Rewak writes, "perhaps the most likeable person in the book, for he is always entirely honest with his feelings"[26]—calls Ralph to inform him of Jay's death. With significant irony, Ralph's conversation is never heard and barely reported; Andrew's comments afterwards, though, are clear: "Talking to that fool is like trying to put socks on an octopus" (183).

In the middle of their grieving process, the family members become very much aware of a "presence" in the house, each one coming to a feeling of someone "never for an instant in one place. It was in the next room, it was in the kitchen, it was in the dining room" (185). In guarded seconds with Andrew, Mary shows her intensity about his death: "it simply felt like Jay. . . . I just mean it felt like his presence" (187). Later, as they listen for additional sounds, Mary remarks that Jay has gone to see the children in their bedroom for the last time. She feels his "presence" in the room, "of his strength, of virility, of helplessness, and of pure calm" (190). He leaves, as he came, quietly and with his duty done, and Mary accepts her loss: "God help me to *realize* it" (191). The family members resume their grief individually and collectively and then leave; Andrew, the family poet, reflects on God's order of life, Jay's death, and his own personal sense of loss. In the early morning hours, walking home, he "remembers" the words of the hymn, "*above thy deep and dreamless sleep, the silent stars go by*" (207). In past years, those words were ones of comfort, but now death interrupts, and his belief in people, in his own continuity, in the justice and mercy of God and in his own hard wish to know God, are shattered. In the house, meantime, Mary and Hannah go to bed, and latter's heart and mind empty and heavy, the former accepting the finality of Jay's death and her own faith in God: "Thy will be done" (211).

In the last three interludes before Part 3, Agee's mirror to the past illuminates, in the first scene, the powerful struggle of Rufus to accommodate other boys from the street and the neighborhood, some young, some older, as friends in his life. He sees these boys, either "cocksure" of themselves or attentive, smiling, and curious, as companions growing up. At times they show contempt and amusement as they use his name in a chorus ditty: "Uh-Rufus, Uh-Rastus, Uh-Johnson, Uh-Brown/uh-What ya gonna do when the rent comes round?" (217). Bewildered and hurt, he asks his parents about his name, and Mary replies that, while the "colored" people use the name, "it was your great-grandfather Lynch's and it's a name to be proud of" (219). Rufus is not convinced altogether, but his identity and position with the boys is partially solved when he sings for them in his own childlike fashion: "I'm a little busy bee, busy bee, busy bee, / I'm a little busy bee, singing in the clover" (223). As he dances and sings he watches the faces of the boys, the older ones "restrained and smiling," the middle-sized boys with faces of "contempt." In the second scene, more in association with Agee's sensibilities, the countryside provides pastoral beauty. The family is driving into the back country, the deep, hill country, a timeless place with its history but very little present. The central figure is Rufus's great-great-grandmother, whose longevity, as Coles writes, "is beyond any meaning of age most of us know. . . . "[27] Agee's description is a composite of mood, picture, tone, color, and rhythm of words, "white bone and black vein . . . brown-splotched skin, the wrinkled knuckles. . . . a red rubber guard ahead of her wedding ring. . . . her eyes . . . as impersonally bright as two perfectly shaped eyes of glass" (238). The family talk has been on the events of history she has lived through: the Civil War, President Lincoln, and even the age and time before and after. Now Rufus, the oldest of her great-great-grandchildren stands before her to close the generational gap; when he kisses her, the bonding is complete. In the third and final scene of the interludes, Rufus rides on a train through the Smokies with Jay, Catherine, and Uncle Ted and Aunt Kate, the latter relatives of a nonentity status from Michigan. The scene has little do with the physical journey but much to do with growing up and the interplay between parents and children and other adults. Ted wants Rufus to whistle at a meal for more cheese, and when he cannot, Mary protests Ted's continuing tease: "I think it's a perfect shame, deceiving a little child like that who's been brought up to trust people. . . ." Jay, Ted, and Kay disagree, and Mary—again on the defensive—concludes: "But he's been brought up to trust older people when they tell him something" (245–46). Agee's unusual picture of childhood innocence, loneliness, and the preparatory moments of experience in life points out not only fears and hopes and a child's naïveté but, more than anything else, Agee's search, a longing and pleading search for an answer to "tell me who I am" (8).

In the final chapters of *A Death in the Family*, Rufus slowly develops a partial understanding of his father's death, not through his mother's somewhat stultified religiosity and interior grief but through Hannah's matured and wise sensibilities and from the knowledge of his father's resurrection, not through the institutional church as personified by Father Jackson but through the positive and reflective words of his Uncle Andrew on the extraordinary events at the cemetery. Rufus is the soloist in these chapters, the conductor, so to speak, of the orchestrated realism and the movements of death, resurrection, and life. Early in Part 3, and on the morning after his father's death, Rufus awakens, picks up his new cap and runs to his parent's bedroom, calling "Daddy! Daddy:" in the room, where he "is brought up short in dismay for his father was not there" (249). Mary, haggard and sleepless, tells both Rufus and Catherine that their father has gone to heaven and would not be coming back. Rufus, with his child's intuition, reacts instantly: "Is Daddy dead?" Ironically, he says the word that no one else, up to this point, can utter, and all at once the details of the room and his own sharpened senses confirm Jay's death, i.e., "a rubbed spot in the rose-patterned carpet," and "a tangle of brown beads and a little cross," his mother's labored breathing, even the "grim, iron cry" (252) of the streetcar.

Later, Rufus turns to Hannah for details of his father's death. He asks the question his mother would or could not answer: "Who hurt him," and when Hannah looks shocked, he adds: "Mama said he got hurt so bad God put him to sleep" (258). At this point in the family grieving, in their own individual landscapes of internal change, the family members' age, vision, depth, and understanding separate Mary and Hannah, the former grieving to herself and unable to communicate a significant life-changing event to her children, the latter grieving for all the family and concerned that the children understand to the best of their abilities what has happened to Jay. Hannah's explanation is clear: "Your father was thrown from the auto. . . . the only mark on his whole body . . . was right here," she said as she pressed "the front of her forefinger to the point of her chin" (259–60). The blue chin mark, at the family viewing, is another key to Jay's connection to each member, their positive memories of him as he was in life without bodily disfigurement. Rufus understands Hannah and prepares for school although he is told he must remain home until after the funeral. What seems important in these opening chapters of Part 3 is that Rufus accepts the death in an unwieldy way but begins a reconstruction of his own interior landscape. He is proud of his father, and even when he encounters boys on the sidewalk outside his house who tell him of the newspaper accounts of Jay's death, he equates pride with death, the death of his father, and he knows that Jay's spirit is always present and will always be a part of his life.

As this rhythm of a new life without his father begins to awaken in Rufus, a jarring note sounds with the appearance of Father Jackson, the representative of Mary's church, all the way from Chattanooga. Agee's "remembrance" of Jackson is moody, stark and black, completely different from the way Jay and Andrew remember him; the words describing Jackson, while reconciling fear and awe on the part of Rufus and Catherine, are incongruities to personal grief itself: "a black glaring collar . . . long shallow hat. . . . he had a long, sharp bluish chin. . . . He carried a small, shining black suitcase. . . . disconcerted . . . displeased" (291). To the children, the minister is not the epitome of their father at all, even though now he sits in their father's chair and smiles above them, resting his eyes on a picture of Jesus as "a little boy . . . talking to all the wise men in the temple" (292). In a short scene, he conveys to the children his inability to share their grief on their level: "Children must not stare at their elders . . . that is ill-bred." Both children want to know about the words "stare . . . elders . . . ill-bred" (292). He chastises them for staring at people and wants them instead "to learn to be little ladies and little gentlemen . . ." (293).

In the final sections of the book, chapters 18 through 20, the grief of the family reaches a climactic pitch as each individual prepares to view Jay's body. The somberness, the blackness, the gravity of the day are momentarily brushed aside for Mary because she has confined herself to her own room, and now is the time to put on her veil and join her family: "Without either desiring to see her face, or caring how it looked, she saw it had changed: through the deep clear veil her gray eyes watched her gray eyes watch her through the deep clear veil" (305). For the viewing, Agee provides detailed imagery of

Jay's "head, his arms, suit" through the eyes of Rufus: "He had his look of faint impatience, the chin strained a little upward . . . the small trendings of a frown . . . the arch of the nose. . . . most of all, there was indifference" (307). In another catalog of features, the bent arm, the angled wrist, the composed head, the dark nostrils, the brushed hair, and the blue marks of the lip and chin (308) confirmed that indifference to Rufus. His father was gone; he would never return.

Rufus was not allowed to attend the funeral, where services were minimal because Jay had not been baptized in the church, but he sees the coffin carried to the hearse. As the procession prepares to start, a "streetcar moved past and they could see heads turning through its windows and a man took off his hat" (323). The streetcar, for the final time, carries people on with their lives, a symbol to remind the Follets that they, too, must now go on with their lives. After the funeral, Andrew takes Rufus for a walk to describe the burial; just before internment, a beautiful butterfly settled on the coffin "just rested there, right over the breast, and stayed there, just barely making his wings breathe like a heart" (334). Andrew paused and then added that, when the coffin reached the bottom earth, the sun came out and the butterfly "flew up out of that—hole in the ground, straightup into the sky so high I couldn't even see him any more" (335). Rufus felt good about Jay now; in fact, "lying there in the darkness did not matter much" (335). Andrew, commenting on the incomplete burial service by the church and Father Jackson, says, "That—that butterfly has got more of God in him than Jackson will ever see for the rest of eternity" (337). The darkness, though, is finally gone, and Andrew and Rufus walk home in silence. The death in a "remembered" family is now complete; in the landscape of the day—bright, clear, sunny and alive—the joy, the sorrow, the hope, and the love are shared in tender intimacy and resolution.

*A Death in the Family*, for both its simplicity and complexity, is a novel for all times, a story of shared experiences in facing the rich and mysterious event of death, unequalled by many other novels of the 1950s. While Norman Mailer, J. D. Salinger, Saul Bellow, and Tennessee Williams were writing of alienation and the deficiencies of human nature, Agee proclaimed the values, aspirations, and ideals of the rural southern small town and the hopes and dreams of families in "place and time." More important, though, and regardless of the setting, the novel addresses the universal questions of life, death, and resurrection through Agee's "precise" language in fine details, exquisite images, the symbols of "remembrance" and "memory," and the extraordinary ability to go beyond the page and to become one with the word. Music and mood flow from page to page and from chapter to chapter through the musical and poetic experiences of verbal orchestration. The "belling" streetcar, as a leading symbol of life, begins in "Knoxville" and ends at Jay's funeral, and it reminds the narrator and the "remembered" family of the frailty of time and life. The great beat, the heart of the novel, though, is the continuous landscape of family, the vision of continuity, and the meaning of life, death, and love.

## Notes

1.   Richard Hayes, "Rhetoric of Splendor," *Commonweal,* 12 Sept. 1958, 591.
2.   Kenneth Seib, *James Agee: Promise and Fulfillment* (Pittsburgh: U of Pittsburgh P, 1968), 90–91.
3.   Ibid., 92.
4.   Mark Doty, *Tell Me Who I Am: James Agee's Search for Selfhood* (Baton Rouge: Louisiana State UP, 1981), xii.
5.   Robert Phelps, Preface, *Letters of James Agee to Father Flye* (New York: Braziller, 1962), 1.
6.   Wilbur Frohock, *The Novel of Violence in America* (Dallas: Southern Methodist UP, 1957), 212.
7.   Dwight Macdonald, *Against the American Grain* (New York: Vintage, 1965), 152.
8.   J. A. Ward, *American Silences: The Realism of James Agee, Walker Evans, and Edward Hopper* (Baton Rouge: Louisiana State UP, 1985).
9.   Robert Coles, *Irony in the Mind's Eye* (Charlottesville: UP of Virginia, 1974), 61.
10.  William John Rewak, "The Shadow and the Butterfly: James Agee's Treatment of Death," diss., U of Minnesota, 1970, 198.
11.  Ibid., 198.
12.  Elizabeth Drew, *Poetry: A Modern Guide to Its Understanding and Enjoyment.* (New York: Norton, 1959), 211–12.
13.  "Knoxville: Summer of 1915," *Partisan Review* 5 (Aug.–Sept. 1938): 25.
14.  James Agee, *A Death in the Family* (New York: McDowell, Obolensky, 1957). Hereafter all pages numbers that refer to this edition will be cited parenthetically in the text.

15. Peter Ohlin, *Agee* (New York: Obolensky, 1966), 43.

16. Drew, *Poetry: A Modern Guide*, 211.

17. Macdonald, *Against the American Grain*, 146.

18. Jeanne Concannon, "The Poetry and Fiction of James Agee: A Critical Analysis," diss., U of Minnesota, 1968, 131.

19. David Johnson, "Notes, Barber: Knoxville: 'Summer, 1915,'" for Samuel Barber's "Knoxville: Summer of 1915," Columbia Records, 1963 (ML5843), qtd. Charles Mayo, "James Agee: His Literary Life and Work," diss., George Peabody College for Teachers, 1969, 157–58 and fn. 105. The author of this chapter is deeply grateful to Robert Bailey, Department of Music, Bethel College, Minnesota, for his help in the interpretation of this composition.

20. *Major British Writers*, ed. G. B. Harrison (New York: Harcourt, 1959), 25.

21. *Letters of James Agee to Father Flye* (New York: Braziller, 1962), 46–47.

22. Concannon, "The Poetry and Fiction of James Agee," 127.

23. Rewak, "The Shadow and the Butterfly," 236.

24. Ibid., 221.

25. Ohlin, *Agee*, 201.

26. Rewak, "The Shadow and the Butterfly," 217.

# Urban and Rural Balance in
## *A Death in the Family*

*Victor A. Kramer*

## I

A DEATH IN THE FAMILY, a very private book, is autobiographical since it is about the death of James Agee's father, yet it is a book
that expands into the public realm because of its exploration of the
country-city conflict central to American experience from post–Civil
War days to the present. The central significance of this conflict in
Agee's book results from his personal experiences, for he was born
in Knoxville, Tennessee, in 1909 when that city, though a town of
only thirty thousand, was rapidly becoming an urban center. Still,
Knoxville during those years possessed enough of a rural flavor to
remain clearly countrified in Agee's mind during his subsequent
years in New York City.[1] His fictionalization of the crucial period in
his life when his father died also documents aspects of a period when
many American lives were still determined by both the rural and town
backgrounds of their families. *A Death in the Family* is, therefore, much
more than a private remembrance because it so clearly reflects the
period when so much of American culture was balanced between
country and city.

When Agee wrote this autobiographical novel he attempted to
catch the flavor of the time when his own family, with ties to both the
rural past and the urban future, was in a state of tension. Interest-
ingly, the novel reflects distrust of an affection for both country and

city. Agee evokes a moment in America's history when it was poised
between a knowledge of a simpler past (or one that appeared to be)
and the more demanding present. The novel is unusual because Agee
attempts to document that past without the philosophical implica-
tions of writers—ranging from Norris and Dreiser to Hemingway and
Faulkner—who have a naturalistic vein in their fiction. Agee also attempts to suggest the beauty of a time past without being sentimental, and yet the result is a lament for a loss of the balanced qualities
that once made up the earlier moment in his life, a loss brought
about by the absorption of country people into cities.

Agee had already begun to write about his memories of Knoxville while he was a sixteen-year-old student at Phillips Exeter Academy in New Hampshire. Clearly at that early time his father's death
haunted him.[2] Significantly, his "Knoxville: Summer of 1915," often
assumed to be part of *A Death in the Family*, was already written in
1936, when Agee was only twenty-seven years old. "Knoxville" is a poetic sketch, largely about Agee's family, and especially his father. By
1937 Agee had also written a screenplay, "The House," in which he
chose as setting a city about the size of "Knoxville or Chattanooga,"
and as might be expected, his imagined house resembles his grand-
parents' home in Knoxville, and a father is notably absent. Similarly,
when Agee recalled earlier autobiographical experiences related to
remembrances in *Let Us Now Praise Famous Men*, his mind flashed back
to years when he had been a fatherless adolescent in Knoxville. All of
Agee's important fiction is autobiographical, and it progresses back-
ward to his earliest remembered years. The book preceding *A Death
in the Family*, *The Morning Watch*, is an evocation of a high point of
religious emotion for a boy of twelve, and its setting is St. Andrew's,
the mountain school, near Sewannee, Tennessee, where Agee was a
student for five years.[3] Preceding that work in composition is the
little-known "1928 Story," which is set in that year, an autobiographical remembrance from the point of view of the mature artist (Agee
in the late 1940s) who recalls his earlier hopes and aspirations.[4]

As Agee the writer grew older he became more aware of how he
had been formed under the influence of his mother and in the absence of a father who had close country ties. His father, Hugh James
Agee, had come of a mountain family, and he embodied many of the

rural qualities of persons who had left farms and become urbanized. Agee's mother came of a different and more urban background. She was the daughter of a prominent businessman, and she was a university graduate. She was interested in art, music, and even more significantly, the Episcopalian church. One extremely important difference between Agee's parents was the interest in formal religion that was fundamental for the mother, yet not apparently of much importance for Agee's father.

In *A Death in the Family* the religion (or religiosity) of the fictional mother is a basic ingredient in her reaction to the death of her husband. Her reliance upon the church, symbolized harshly by the fictional Father Jackson, stands both structurally and thematically in conflict with the early parts of the book when the true father is present. Especially for the children, something seems unnatural and frightening in a man like Father Jackson, a letter-of-the-law-religious who refuses to provide a complete burial service for Jay, the father, because he is not a believer. The character Rufus and his sister sense they cannot trust Father Jackson the minute he appears at the door to comfort their mother. In contrast to this cold priest, Agee draws portraits of several strong country men. Among the most important of those men who retain a likable rural character is Walter Starr, who chooses to let the children watch the casket be carried out of the house on the day of the funeral. Starr functions as a symbol of independence and independent judgment.

Rufus's father is appealing precisely because he is independently strong, but it is apparent that Rufus will become more reliant upon guidance from his mother and organized religion after the father's death. And the individualism, naturalness, and openness—essentially rural qualities of the father—will be missed and become only something later to imagine.

The fictional parents of *A Death in the Family* had experienced a tension in their marriage, "a Gulf" that had, Agee imagines, only recently begun to close. This marriage was growing into a strong bond, which apparently would have been beneficial to all the family members. The father's death abruptly breaks that balance, and the urban, genteel qualities of the mother promise to become dominant; Jay's active contribution to the rearing of his children is lost with his death.

The same might well be said of the cultural ties with a rural America that most urban people have lost during the twentieth century. It is no accident, therefore, that Agee lavishes detail upon the opening chapter of this novel for it is here that the contrast between father and mother which sets the tone for the book is evoked, and the quiet presence of the father is, as well, emphasized.

Just as for the characters of his novel, Agee's own life was inevitably formed because of decisions made by his mother in the absence of his father. Her awareness that her young son needed the influence of male teachers was partially responsible for his enrollment at St. Andrew's School near Sewanee; and her interest in religion simultaneously had definite effects on Agee's own religious formation.[5] After five years at St. Andrew's and a year of high school in Knoxville, he attended Phillips Exeter Academy, and then Harvard College. Graduating at the peak of the Great Depression, Agee landed a job on the staff of *Fortune* magazine, and his subsequent frustration in writing unsigned pieces for *Fortune* and *Time*, film criticism for *The Nation*, and, later, screenplays before his early death, is emblematic of problems many American writers face. He was in some basic ways displaced.

Agee's work as a professional journalist in New York City, a place as different as imaginable from the Tennessee mountains where his father had been reared, did not allow him sufficient time to do "his own writing," but each of the substantial prose works that he did complete are noteworthy because they demonstrate that he never lost his affection for the Tennessee and Knoxville of his earliest years. Agee's major work also reflects his awareness of how his important formative influences were a blending of urban and rural forces. His best writing was therefore always in part the result of his personal experience: his childhood, his ties with Knoxville and the mountains of Tennessee. For instance his recognition that, given a different set of circumstances, he might have been born into a life similar to that of the tenant farmers he wrote about in *Let Us Now Praise Famous Men* becomes a basic part of that work's design. Similarly, *The Morning Watch* could never have been written without Agee's memories of that country school where he spent five years; and finally, *A Death in the Family* is a novel that expands outward to represent many lives. To understand to what degree the book is autobiographical one need only know that among the manuscript notes are detailed lists of particular moments and events recalled from the days surrounding the father's funeral, much of which was also fictionalized.[6] The closing sequence of the book where Rufus's uncle tells him about the butterfly that settled on the coffin as it was lowered into the ground was "vaguely" remembered by Agee.[7] The same certainly is the case with many other episodes, such as the teasing of Rufus by older boys and the details of the day of the funeral. Still other parts of excluded manuscript for *A Death in the Family* seem to be based either on memories of incidents recalled or upon incidents that Agee must have remembered from hearing others speak. The "Surprise" chapter, included in the 1968 gathering with other materials in *The Texas Quarterly* would be an example. Father James Harold Flye commented that Agee's book could never have been finished because its method was one of memory.

## II

As Agee was first planning *A Death*, it appears that he wanted to rely upon a technique similar to that employed in *Famous Men*. That is, he would write only what he could remember. This is especially true of the opening and closing sections of the book and the interchapter materials, which fall outside the main chronological sequence. But this novel also developed out of a larger conflict; in a fundamental way it was Agee's mode of simultaneously remembering the past and getting away from the horrors of the present. He wrote much of the text that became this novel in the late 1940s, a time when he was especially disturbed by the use of the atomic bomb as well as the problem of how individuals can survive in a mass society. Both "Dedication Day" and "Scientists and Tramps" are from this period. In "1928 Story," written at approximately the same time as *A Death* was begun, Agee begins by outlining the disappointment and frustration his speaker feels in not having written as much, or as well, as he might have. In "1928 Story" such statements flow into a remembrance of earlier times, and the speaker is able to catch the beauty (and awkwardness) of earlier moments.

In *A Death in the Family* Agee also took very simple events from his childhood and then allowed his imagination to play over them. Some parts of his remembrance are therefore chronologically months or years in advance of the father's death. With such reference points it was possible for him to reconstruct the domestic love that enveloped the young Rufus, a love that combined country and city attitudes.

Agee was only six years old when his father died; thus while his book is definitely written to honor his father, it is also an attempt to catch a moment then three decades in the past. As Agee matured, he came to realize that particular events and places in his childhood neighborhood had been experienced both by him and his father. For instance, the railroad viaduct, which today still bridges the valley between the business center of Knoxville and residential areas, was a specific place that Agee associated with his father. The bridge is very carefully described in the fictional account of Rufus and Jay, and the description reveals the method of the entire book. Details about the remembered past are evoked through careful attention to the "dignity of actuality." Rufus recalls how "Whenever they walked downtown and walked back home, in the evenings, they always began to walk more slowly, from about the middle of the viaduct, and as they came near [their] corner they walked more slowly still, but with purpose. . . ."[8] Through this specific attention to details of place, such a passage suggests how Rufus intuitively sensed the homesickness of his father.

Readers of this novel usually first recall the sketch "Knoxville: Summer of 1915," which was chosen by David McDowell as an opening for the book. Its dominant tone is one of nostalgia for an earlier quiet time; and it, as already suggested, is one of several autobiographical or reminiscent pieces about Tennessee that were written in the 1930s. Another is an experimental poem, entitled "In Memory of My Father,"[9] in which some of the same imagery employed in the novel is used; the poetic remembrance of a small child, going to sleep and comforted by the parent, is an image suggesting all children in similar circumstances. Agee's 1936 sketch, "Knoxville: Summer of 1915," similarly does an economical job of evoking an atmosphere like that which Rufus and his father enjoy, such as at the beginning of the novel when they go to the movies and later walk home together. In the "Knoxville" sketch, inserted as an introduction, a time of harmony with nature is imagined: the cities' noises are blended with natural ones. But the mood that actually generated the novel is evident in an excluded passage that I have edited and entitled "Dream Sequence." This is the real introduction to the novel. In it the tension between country and city is clearly evident. Edited nine years after the novel's publication, Agee's "Dream" begins as nightmare and suggests that only through a work of art can any lasting harmony be achieved. It is necessary for the artist first to exorcise the nightmare of urban life if the peacefulness of a remembrance like *A Death in the Family* is to be created.

"Dream Sequence" is a sketch recording the nightmare of a narrator (very much like Agee) who recalls how he found himself on a crowded city street—perhaps New York, perhaps Chattanooga—but then obviously Knoxville: "The town had certainly changed. It wasn't as he remembered it from childhood, nor did he like its looks as well as his memories of it. . . . Even the heat and sunlight of the weather was different, it was the weather of a bigger, worse, more proud and foolish city. . . ."[10] The narrator then relates how he saw a group of people doing something horrible to someone, and upon approaching that crowd he knew the figure was John the Baptist and that he was being stoned. The narrator decided a proper burial was in order, and he began that chore. He began pulling the corpse down the sweltering and then freezing streets—symbolism that suggests the passing of years. And as time passed, the terrain became more and more familiar. In both this "Dream" and in the opening section of the novel, Agee recalls the outcroppings of limestone common to the landscape of Knoxville. A visitor to Agee's old neighborhood in Knoxville would notice the same outcroppings today.

Two things become clearer to Agee's dreamer. First, he was getting closer to his old childhood neighborhood, and this was the atmosphere he and his father used to enjoy in their privacy late at night: "The corner was where he used to sit with his father and it was there of all times and places that he had known his father loved him. . . . and his father had come out of the wilderness." And secondly, if the man was John the Baptist, he was somehow also the narrator's father, and he, the Christ, had failed his father. The question is how that failure could be (at least partially) rectified. The answer is to go back into those years, by way of a work of art, and to do honor to the memory of the father by evoking as much of those times as possible. This became the basic method, and accomplishment, of Agee's novel. To remember, or to infer, as much as possible, and thereby through art to impose order upon the chaos of life, its disruptions and its memories.

The last pages of the "Dream Sequence" possess a calmness similar to the opening of the book. Agee's return to the calmness of his childhood, interrupted by the father's death, is made, therefore, by way of the horrors of contemporary life, an urban life symbolized by a maddened crowd. Agee's homage to this father, then, seems to be both a recapitulation of what he remembered and a symbolic statement about all who are drawn to the city.

There is both terror and a large amount of nostalgia in what Agee decided to write about, yet it is only through nostalgia that it is possible for a writer of fiction to achieve a perspective adequate for such a vision of how rural and urban forces were once in conjunction to form particular moments of domestic love. Agee wanted to do honor to that earlier time. To do so, his memory became as important as his imagination. It is significant to observe that throughout the manuscript for this novel the names of real persons are consistently used. The same is true of much of the manuscript for *The Morning Watch* and *Let Us Now Praise Famous Men*.

Agee wrote in one of the working notes for *A Death in the Family* that Jay, the father, was a "victim of progress." One of the variant sections for the book is a discussion between the parents about the dangers of purchasing an automobile.[11] What better symbol, we might ask, is there for the fragmentation of family? A particular marriage and its love provided an atmosphere for Rufus; and the inference is clearly suggested that the child drew upon the earlier time when rural forces, and the presence of the father, were being blended with city life. Agee and modern American culture and modern Americans, however, seem largely to have lost the strength to be gained from such a blending.

Clearly there is the possibility that, had Agee lived to complete his novel, he would have written more sections stressing his autobiographical remembrances of both country and city. One such excluded section is a two-page sequence in which Rufus recalls how his father used to spit in the fireplace—much to the horror of the mother. After she had instructed Jay not to do such a thing in front of Rufus, Rufus continued to observe Jay doing it, but only when the mother was absent.[12]

When Rufus is in the presence of either of his parents, or when he thinks about them, Agee stresses the contrast between them, yet also their contribution of qualities that make the child's world secure. One section of the novel is, appropriately, a stream-of-consciousness monologue in which the child muses about the differences he senses between his parents: "She wore dresses, his father wore pants. Pants were what he wore too, but they were short and soft" (100). Similar passages are incorporated throughout the text.

It is the combination of mother and father, with their differing attitudes, that allows Rufus to feel at ease. Rufus remembers a motoring trip to visit the father's relatives: *"After the dinner the babies and all the children except Rufus were laid out on the beds to take their naps, and his mother thought that he ought to lie down too, but his father said no, why did he need to, so he was allowed to stay up"* (227). Similarly, when Rufus is first introduced to his great-great-grandmother, and he kisses her, the mother voices concern and his father says "Let her be" (240). Jay will have Rufus experience as much of the diverse world as possible, and he tries not to be overly protective. In another episode Aunt Hannah senses that the cap Rufus wants is correct for a boy who wants to be grown up. A year earlier Rufus had asked his mother for a cap but suffered a rebuff when she refused. We can understand with Rufus that, if Jay took him shopping, "his father wouldn't mind" (14) if he had such a cap, even though his mother "wouldn't want him to have a cap, yet." Hannah reflects that "Mary would have conniption fits" over Rufus's choice, but "Jay wouldn't mind" (78).

In a related way, during the opening pages of the novel when Jay and Rufus are getting ready to go see a Chaplin movie, Jay enjoys asking "What's wrong with [Charlie]?" "not because he didn't know what she would say, but so she would say it" (11). And then when Rufus and his father go, ritualistically, to the movies they feel all the more enclosed in each others' presence. This fictional father is somewhat rough, a bit coarse, and country. But the boy's mother seems overly genteel; and going to the movies is an escape from her for both father and son. On the walk home Jay stops off at a saloon looking for friends from his home area in the mountains. This is, perhaps, one of the most poignant scenes in the novel because the saloon is both a meeting place and a reminder of the inevitability that the rural connections of the past are impossible to maintain. The many hints throughout this text about Jay's alcoholism (by inference a commentary on Agee's own drinking problems) are another way of commenting on the difficulty of adulthood and change.

Rufus senses that he needs and will need both parents, but he is without such abstract knowledge. Agee, looking back over his own life and his remembrance of those years, also saw the need for the balance provided by both parents and their traditions. Therefore, the picture we are given of Rufus's parents frequently combines their best qualities. Where this is most apparent is the contrast in the scenes where Jay and Mary, separately, sing to Rufus. Jay loved to sing the old country songs that he remembered from childhood. Rufus also realized that sometimes his father joked by talking like a "darky," and *"the way he sang was like a darky too, only when he sang he wasn't joking"* (99–100). Rufus also remembered how his parents sang together and how beautifully his mother's clear voice combined with Jay's, yet he also sensed that when she tried to sound like a country singer she could not do it. Rufus "liked both ways very much and best of all when they sang together and he was there with them, . . ." yet he is suddenly separated from such experience when his father is killed and the boy is thus doomed to his mother's dominant influence.

Throughout the novel it is implied that Jay has accommodated himself to living in the city. The passage describing his journey to his own father's sick bed, the very trip that ironically leads to his death, points up how he must have often felt about aspects of the city. "The city thinned out," Agee wrote, and for a few minutes Jay drove through

> the darkened evidences of that kind of flea-bitten semi-rurality which
> always peculiarly depressed him: mean little homes, and others
> inexplicably new and substantial, set too close together for any satisfy-
> ing rural privacy or use, too far, too shapelessly apart to have adher-
> ence ["coherence" in pencil manuscript] as any kind of community;

> mean little pieces of ill-cultivated land behind them, and alongside the
> road, between them, trash and slash and broken sheds and rained-out
> billboards. . . . (44)

This is the same kind of feeling almost everyone experiences (unconsciously perhaps) as movement from urban to rural is experienced. Such a feeling would have been all the more acute if a rural background were one's origin. Then, it might seem, material progress and faith in institutions—whether governmental or religious—might be increasingly difficult to accept. Seventy years ago, when Agee's father was in his middle thirties, it would have clearly been an even more poignant feeling, and this is what Agee seeks to evoke.

It is also made clear that Agee's fictional family was in the habit of going into the country for Sunday drives. The ferryman who takes Jay across the river recognizes him: "You generally always come o' Sunday's, year womurn, couple o' younguns," and Jay answers with a monosyllabic reply reflecting his country ties: "Yeahp" (45). Jay's wife also clearly senses that Jay feels most comfortable in the country; and when she prepares Jay's breakfast in the early morning of his departure, she does it the way she imagines a mountain woman might.

Another revealing interchange between spouses about family and change occurs in the novel during one of the family trips to visit relatives. On that particular Sunday the parents attempt to figure out how old the great-great-grandmother might be, and Mary comments "—*why she's almost as old as the country, Jay*" (232). Jay's reply suggests an enormous amount about how the parents think. He immediately meditates on the natural world—the geological fact of the mountains; but the mother thinks of the nation's government. Dealing in abstract concepts is not Jay's ordinary mode of thought. He deals more immediately with the concrete, and it is for such reasons that he enjoys being with Rufus and singing old songs. There are many manuscript variants from the section about singing that demonstrate Agee's fascination and interest in this subject. During one of his evenings of song Jay recalls how his own mother used to sing to him (and how those times are gone),[13] yet how through one's children they can be repeated, at least a little bit: "Just one way, you do get back home.

You have a boy or a girl of your own and now and then you remember, and you know how they feel. . . ." (94)

## III

There is yet another way to "get back home," and that is the artist's. In one of the working notes for the novel Agee recalled that on one of the mornings surrounding his father's funeral he and his sister were taught how to read the comics—arms just so, legs up, and bellies on the floor, and he added a comment that such actions implied archetypal actions performed by those unaware of what they were doing. Agee's entire fictionalization is archetypal in this manner. Thus various parts of this book work similarly to suggest either the fragmentation of family or the loss of rural virtues. A motif buried in this text, yet referred to regularly in the working notes, is Agee's fascination with Rufus's inability to fight and Jay's subsequent embarrassment about this lack. The scene about the child's wandering the Knoxville streets the morning after his father's death symbolically enacts what all must feel in such situations. In this sense Agee's concerns are archetypal. His novel is a meditation about a wider pattern of all fathers absorbed by the city, then senselessly killed, with their families then accordingly destined to be formed in their absence.

The central theme of Agee's book is domestic love—a subject that seems particularly unpromising for a novelist in the middle part of the twentieth century. But delicate domestic love, which has been experienced by millions and millions of families, is what holds Agee's remembrance together. The family has always provided comfort and nurture, but in a society like today's, the family seems best described by Henry Adams in his delineation of the centrifugal forces generated by the society. Family members spin away from each other as external activities become more pronounced. However, each action and gesture of love is unique, and as these individual acts are performed, they have value within a unique framework. It was such a realization, along with the conviction that city forces were becoming stronger, that must have prompted Agee to "go back into those years."

The precision that Agee achieved in the writing of this book has sometimes been compared to uses of the camera; it is not, as we have seen, a novel in the ordinary sense. Agee's language and point of view often rely heavily upon visual remembrance of actions. In a very real sense we might argue that Agee's prose is more akin to a documentary than to fictionalization, and yet, significantly, the precise focus on details also makes this a book about Agee's life *and* everybody's life as suggested by this particular moment of balance. The entire first chapter, the details provided about Jay's departure at three in the morning, the definiteness of Aunt Hannah and Rufus's shopping trip, and the details of the funeral itself are only a few of the many places where Agee's descriptive powers focus upon such minute particularities. It is precisely because Agee so respected his remembered world that his fiction was easily adapted into a drama and film. In the play and film as well as in the text for the novel, one is assured that one is witness to a way of life that is passing. It has sometimes been remarked that Agee's book is not a novel at all but really a long poem similar to the multifaceted remembrances of *Let Us Now Praise Famous Men*. This is correct, and Agee's lyrical writing attests to moments that would fade away with no memorial if he chose not to write of them, but because he evokes particularities, he catches aspects of that earlier era. Ironically, the Agee home had been razed by the time the film *All The Way Home* was made in the middle 1960s, and in its place in Knoxville were "The James Agee Apartments," which have now become condominiums.

As one is reminded of the change that a city like Knoxville has undergone, one may be able to focus on an earlier time when so many opposing forces were clearly still in productive tension. The little town imagined in this novel was small enough that, after Jay's death, Mary's family could simply walk over to her house. Yet, as has been suggested, this was already a city where Jay could not feel completely at home. Throughout the novel the sounds of railroad cars interrupt domestic privacy and quiet. And, at the end of the chapter, when Jay has departed to visit his sick father, Agee ends with the sentence "A streetcar passed; Catherine cried" (54), implying how the city, with its trolleys and automobiles, was affecting lives.

Agee's text could be examined in far more detail. How advertising, movies, the church, undertakers, neighbors, railroads, relatives, and visitors function within this story is all revealed in a subtle way within this grouping of remembrances. Agee imagined all this; remembered much of it; lived all of it as he reconstructed it. His job was to show how any one moment of the past was a moment in balance because of the interaction of many different forces.

Agee wrote that Jay the fictional character was a "victim of progress." He is, and so is the family, which might have developed differently had the father lived and been able to exert influence during the formation of Rufus the boy beyond his first few years. But Jay died, as did that era of American history—but not without inspiring the work of art that was fashioned into *A Death in the Family*. Through the novelist's art that somewhat more balanced era remains alive.

Agee learned to appreciate the universal by means of a careful rendition of the particular. All of his best writing works this way. Each moment in life and history and imagination quickly blends into others and into quite different moments. Yet each moment is to be honored. The text for Agee's unfinished *A Death in the Family* is, therefore, a book that functions on several levels at once: it is Agee's memorial; it is his examination of self; it is a picture of a particular era when urban and rural were blended; it is an archetypal rendering of what all persons learn, live, and love.

## Notes

This chapter is an expanded and revised version of "Urban and Rural Tension in *A Death in the Family*," which appeared in *Agee and Actuality: Artistic Vision in His Work*. Reprinted with the permission of Whitston Publishing Company.

1. See Agee's story about the Tennessee Valley Authority, in which he describes Knoxville (*Fortune* 11 [May 1935]: 93–98 and 140–53).
2. For instance, Agee published a poem about a widow on Christmas Eve in *The Phillips Exeter Monthly* 30 (May 1926): 180.
3. See Victor A. Kramer, "James Agee's Unpublished Manuscript and His Emphasis on Religious Emotion in *The Morning Watch*," *Tennessee Studies in Literature* 17 (1972): 159–64.
4. "1928 Story" is part of "Agee in the Forties: Unpublished Poetry and Fiction," ed. Victor A. Kramer, *Texas Quarterly* 11 (Spring 1968): 23–27.
5. Mrs. Agee published a book of religious poems while she was in residence at St. Andrew's. See the discussion of Laura Tyler Agee's *Songs of the Way* (St. Andrew's, TN: n.p., 1922) in Charles W. Mayo's doctoral

dissertation "James Agee: His Literary Life and Work," Peabody Inst., 1969, 22+ff.

6.  Peter Ohlin's *Agee* (New York: Obolensky, 1966) discusses the novel in terms of how Agee transfigures reality. While Ohlin had no access to manuscript materials and does not mention the urban-rural themes in the book, his discussion does provide insight into how Agee fictionalizes ordinary experience.

7.  Agee's working notes for *A Death in the Family*, now at the Harry Ransom Humanities Research Center of the University of Texas at Austin, show that he, at least early in the book's composition, thought about incorporating many details about family outings. The James Agee Trust has granted permission for my use of these materials. See Victor A. Kramer, "*A Death in the Family* and Agee's Projected Novel," *Proof* 3 (1973): 139–54.

8.  James Agee, *A Death in the Family* (New York: McDowell, Obolensky, 1957), 18. All subsequent references are within parentheses in the text.

9.  *Collected Poems of James Agee* (Boston: Houghton, 1968), 59.

10. "Dream Sequence" is part of "Agee in the Forties," 38–46.

11. See Victor A. Kramer, "Premonition of Disaster: An Unpublished Section for Agee's *A Death in the Family*," *Costerus* ns 1 (1974): 83–93.

12. Kramer, "*A Death in the Family* and Agee's Projected Novel," 149–50.

13. Victor A. Kramer, "Agee's Use of Regional Material in *A Death in the Family*," *Appalachian Journal* 1 (Autumn 1972): 72–80, includes a variant version of this section.

# Agee: A Bibliography
# of Secondary Sources

## Mary Moss

### A Note on the Bibliography

ALTHOUGH JAMES AGEE at his death left behind a relatively small corpus of work (only three books of his were published during his lifetime), his writing has continued to excite critical inquiry. Since his death, five collections and a novel have been published—attesting to the enduring power of his writing. Because Agee's works cover so many genres—journalism, film, fiction, poetry—they pose peculiar problems for the literary researcher. Standard searches through the MLA bibliography turn up only a portion of the commentary on Agee and his writing. Much of the secondary material published on Agee appears in popular sources—sources not always listed in scholarly indexes. Because Agee is both an observer and himself an object of popular culture, it seems appropriate to examine alternate sources.

I am indebted to the efforts of two previous Agee bibliographers: Nancy Lyman Huse, *John Hersey and James Agee: A Reference Guide* (1978), and Steven Aulicino, whose article in *Bulletin of Bibliography* brings the search up through 1981. The present bibliography, which covers the years through 1988, incorporates and, in a few cases, emends the two preceding bibliographies. This bibliography also includes reviews of Tad Mosel's play *All the Way Home,* based on Agee's *A Death in the Family.* I have included these reviews because I think they demonstrate the chord that Agee's work touched in people.

Whenever possible, I have used standard MLA abbreviations for periodicals. Readers not familiar with these should consult the master list of abbreviations printed in each yearly installment of the MLA index. Where no abbreviation exists, I have given the complete name of the periodical in question. Items that I have not personally examined are marked with an asterisk.

Agee, Joel. *Twelve Years: An American Boyhood in East Germany.* New York: Farrar, 1981.

*Reviews*

Coles, Robert. "Growing Up East German." *New York Review of Books* 16 July 1981: 49–50.

Marsh, Pamela. "The East Germans—Close Up." *Christian Science Monitor* 22 July 1981: 17.

McDowell, Edwin. "James and Joel Agee: Like Father, Like Son?" *New York Times* 25 Apr. 1981: 11.

Mysak, Joe. Review. *National Review* 27 Nov. 1981: 1435.

Reed, J. D. "Young Misfit." *Time* 11 May 1981: 90.

Richardson, Jack. "Growing Up German." *New York Times Book Review* 26 Apr. 1981: 12+.

Review. *Atlantic* 247.6 (1981): 101.

Agee, Mia, and Gerald Locklin. "Faint Lines in a Drawing of Jim." Madden 153–62.

"Agee on Agee." *Newsweek* 23 July 1962: 75.

Review of *Agee on Film* [vol. 1]. *Booklist* 55 (1958): 207.

Review of *Agee on Film* [vol. 1]. *New Yorker* 13 Dec. 1958: 215–16.

Review of *Agee on Film,* vol. 2. *Booklist* 56 (1960): 473.

Review of *Agee on Film,* vol. 2. *New York Herald Tribune Book Review* 15 May 1960: 12.

Aiken, Charles S. "The Transformation of James Agee's Knoxville." *Geographical Review* 73 (1983): 150–65.

Allister, Mark Christopher. "Encounters with Unimagined Existence: Documentary and Autobiography in Recent American Prose." *DAI* 46 (1986): 3717A. Diss. U of Washington.

——. "Seeing, Knowing, and Being: James Agee's *Let Us Now Praise Famous Men.*" *Pst* 9 (1986): 86–102.

Alpert, Hollis. "The Terror on the River." *Saturday Review* 13 Aug. 1955: 21.

"An American Classic." *Newsweek* 5 Sept. 1960: 74.

Ashdown, Paul, ed. Introduction. *James Agee: Selected Journalism.* Knoxville: U of Tennessee P, 1985. xiii–xliv.

——. "James Agee's Magazine Journalism." *Seventh Annual Communications Research Symposium: A Proceedings.* Ed. Michael W. Singletary. [Knoxville]: U of Tennessee, May, 1984.

Auden, W. H. Letter. *Nation* 159 (1944): 628.

Aulicino, Steven. "James Agee: Secondary Sources, 1935–1981." *BB* 41.2 (1984): 64–72.

Barker, George. "Three Tenant Families." Review of *Let Us Now Praise Famous Men. Nation* 153 (1941): 282.

Barry, Edward. "Wholesome but Difficult Novel of an Adolescent." Review of *The Morning Watch. Chicago Sunday Tribune* 24 June 1951, sec. 4: 4.

Barson, Alfred T. "James Agee: A Study of Artistic Consciousness." *DAI* 30 (1970): 5438A. Diss. U of Massachusetts.

——. *A Way of Seeing: A Critical Study of James Agee.* Amherst: U of Massachusetts P, 1972.

*Review*

Sosnoski, James J. "A Significant Failure." *JGE* 26 (1974): 69–76.


Bazelon, David T. "*Agee on Film.*" Review of *Agee on Film* [vol. 1]. *Village Voice* 24 Dec. 1958: 12+.

Behar, Jack. "James Agee: Notes on the Man and the Work." *UDQ* 13 (1978): 3–15.

——. "James Agee: The World of His Work." *DA* 24 (1964): 4690. Diss. Ohio State U.

——. "On Rod Serling, James Agee, and Popular Culture." *TV as Art: Some Essays in Criticism.* Ed. Patrick. D. Hazard. Champaign IL: NCTE, 1966: 35–63.

Belsches, Alan Thomas. "The Southern Tradition: Five Studies in Memory." *DAI* 44 (1984): 3682A–83A. Diss. U of North Carolina–Chapel Hill.

Benet, W. R. Review of *Permit Me Voyage*. *Saturday Review* 24 Nov. 1934: 314.

Bergreen, Laurence. *James Agee: A Life*. New York: Dutton, 1984. Rpt. New York: Penguin, 1985.

*Reviews*

Broyard, Anatole. "Taking Life by Storm." *New York Times* 30 June 1984: 12.

French, Phillip. "His Death Gave Life to His Legend." *New York Times Book Review* 8 July 1984: 1+.

Maddocks, Melvin. "Captive Poet." *Time* 12 July 1984: 85.

Maine, Barry. Review. *AL* 57 (1985): 348–49.

Rodman, Selden. "By Guilt Possessed." *New Leader* 6 Aug. 1984: 18–19.

Rose, Lloyd. "Critics Critic." *American Film* Sept. 1984: 57–58.

Rovit, Earl. Review. *Library Journal* 109 (1984): 1236.

Spears, Ross. "Fiction as Life." *YR* 74 (1985): 296–306.

Teachout, Terry. "Nothing Much to Say." *National Review* 22 Feb. 1985: 46–48.

Weber, Ronald. "Through a Glass Darkly." *VQR* 61 (1985): 360–65.

White, Edmund. "Let Us Now Praise." *New Republic* 3 Sept. 1984: 25–28.

Betts, Leonidas. "Unfathomably Mysterious: *Let Us Now Praise Famous Men*." *EJ* 59 (1970): 44+.

"Bibliography." *Harvard Advocate* 105.4 (1972): 49–53.

Bingham, Robert. "Short of a Distant Goal." *Reporter* 25 Oct. 1962: 54+.

Blackshear, Orrilla. Review of *Letters of James Agee to Father Flye*. *Wisconsin Library Bulletin* 58 (1962): 342.

Bluestone, George. *Novels into Film*. Baltimore: Johns Hopkins UP, 1957.

Bornstein, George. "James Agee." *TLS* 18 Aug. 1972: 971.

Breit, Harvey. "Cotton Tenantry." Review of *Let Us Now Praise Famous Men*. *New Republic* 15 Sept. 1941: 348+.

———. "In and Out of Books: Tribute." *New York Times* 22 Apr. 1956: 8.

Brender, R. "The Quiet One: Lyric Poetry of the Fair Deal." *Millennium* 13 (1983–84): 81–97.

Broughton, George, and Panthea Reid Broughton. "Agee and Autonomy." *SHR* 4 (1970): 101–11.

Burger, Nash K. "A Story to Tell: Agee, Wolfe, and Faulkner." *SAQ* 63 (1964): 32–43.

Cades, Linda Jean. "The Theme of Grief in Contemporary Southern American Fiction: A Study of Novels by Faulkner, Agee, Arnow, Styron, Welty, and Percy." *DAI* 44 (1984): 3063A. Diss. U of Maryland.

Cassity, Turner. Review of *Collected Poems of James Agee*. *Poetry* 114 (1969): 409–11.

Chambers, Whitaker. "Agee." *Cold Friday*. Ed. Duncan Norton-Taylor. New York: Random, 1964. 268–71. Rpt. in Madden 150–52.

Chase, Richard. "Sense and Sensibility." *KR* 13 (1951): 688–91.

Chesnick, Eugene. "The Plot against Fiction: *Let Us Now Praise Famous Men*." *SLJ* 4.1 (1971): 48–67.

"Chronology." *Harvard Advocate* 105.4 (1972): 48.

Coleman, John. "On Film." *New Statesman* 11 Oct. 1963: 498–99.

Coles, Robert. "Camera on James Agee." *New Republic* 3 Nov. 1979: 23–28.

———. Review of *Collected Poems*. *Commonweal* 89 (1968): 357.

———. *Irony in the Mind's Life: Essays on Novels by James Agee, Elizabeth Bowen, and George Eliot*. Charlottesville: UP of Virginia, 1974. Rpt. New York: New Directions, 1978.

———. "James Agee's 'Famous Men' Seen Again." *Harvard Advocate* 105.4 (1972): 42–46.

———. "James Agee's Search." *Raritan* 3.1 (1983): 74–100.

———. *That Red Wheelbarrow: Selected Literary Essays*. Iowa City: U of Iowa P, 1988.

Review of *Collected Short Prose of James Agee*. *Christian Century* 86 (1969): 257.

Concannon, Jeanne M. "The Poetry and Fiction of James Agee: A Critical Analysis." *DAI* 30 (1970): 2962A–63A. Diss. U of Minnesota.

Condon, Judith. "James Agee in Paperback." *CQ* 5 (1970): 200–207.

Cooper, Arthur. "Appreciating Agee." *Newsweek* 7 Apr. 1969: 86.

Cort, John C. Review of *Let Us Now Praise Famous Men*. *Commonweal* 34 (1941): 499–500.

Croce, Arlene. "Hollywood and the Monolith." *Commonweal* 69 (1959): 430–33.

Crowther, Bosley. Review of *Agee on Film*. *American Scholar* 29 (1960): 436.

Culp, Mildred L. "Nobody . . . Is Specially Privileged." *Death Education* 2 (1979): 369–80.

Curry, Kenneth. "The Knoxville of James Agee's *A Death in the Family*." *TSL* 14 (1969): 1–14.

———. "Notes on the Text of James Agee's *A Death in the Family*." *PBSA* 64 (1970): 84–99.

Curtis, James C., and Sheila Grannen. "Let Us Now Appraise Famous Photographs: Walker Evans and Documentary Photography." *Wintarthur Portfolio* 15 (1980): 1–23.

da Ponte, Durant. "James Agee: The Quest for Identity." *TSL* 8 (1963): 25–37.

Dardis, Tom. "James Agee: The Man Who Loved the Movies." *American Film* 7 June 1976: 62–67.

———. *Some Time in the Sun*. New York: Scribner, 1976.

*Review*

Snyder, Stephen. "From Words to Images: Five Novelists in Hollywood." *CRèvAs* 8 (1977): 206–13.

———. "Some Time in the Sun: The Hollywood Years of Fitzgerald, Faulkner, Nathanael West, Aldous Huxley, and James Agee." *DAI* 41 (1981): 4392–93A. Diss. Columbia U.

Davis, Louise. "The Agee Story: Part One: Two Deaths in the Family." *Nashville Tennessean Magazine* 8 Feb. 1959: 10+.

———. "The Agee Story: Part Two: He Tortured the Thing He Loved." *Nashville Tennessean Magazine* 15 Feb. 1959: 14+.

Review of *A Death in the Family*. *Booklist* 54 (1957): 198.

deFord, Miriam Allen. "Our Own American Inferno." *Humanist* 21 (1961): 55–56.

DeJong, David Cornel. "Money and Rue." *Carleton Miscellany* 6.1 (1965): 50–52.

Dempsey, David. "Praise of Him Was Posthumous." Review of *Letters of James Agee to Father Flye*. *Saturday Review* 11 Aug. 1962: 24–25.

Deutsch, Babette. "The Poet as Social Philosopher." Review of *Permit Me Voyage*. *Survey Graphic* 24 (1935): 134–36.

Dietrichson, Jan W. "Theme and Technique in James Agee's *A Death in the Family*." *American Studies in Scandinavia* [ns] 6 (1973–74): 1–20.

Doty, Mark Allen. "'Tell Me Who I Am': James Agee's Search for Selfhood." *DAI* 39 (1978): 883A. Diss. Indiana U.

———. *Tell Me Who I Am: James Agee's Search for Selfhood*. Baton Rouge: Louisiana State UP, 1981.

Dunlea, William. "Agee and the Writer's Vocation." Review of *Letters of James Agee to Father Flye*. *Commonweal* 76 (1962): 499–500.

Dupee, F. W. "Memories of James Agee." *"The King of the Cats," and Other Remarks on Writers and Writing*. New York: Farrar, 1965. 80–84.

———. "Pride of Maturity." Review of *The Morning Watch*. *Nation* 172 (1951): 400–401.

———. "The Prodigious James Agee." Review of *A Death in the Family*. *New Leader* 9 Dec. 1957: 20–21.

Ellertsen, Peter. "James Agee, the Bomb and Oliver the Cat." *Christian Century* 102 (1985): 709–11.

Elliot, George P. "They're Dead but They Won't Lie Down." Review of *A Death in the Family*. *Hudson Review* 11 (1958–59): 131–40.

Etzkorn, Leo R. Review of *Let Us Now Praise Famous Men*. *Library Journal* 66 (1941): 667.

Evans, Walker. "James Agee in 1936." *Atlantic* 206.1 (1960): 74–75. Rpt.

in Madden 103–7; *Harvard Advocate* 105.4 (1972): 23–24; *Let Us Now Praise Famous Men*. New York: Houghton, 1988. xli–xliv.

"Experiment in Communication." Review of *Let Us Now Praise Famous Men*. *Time* 13 Oct. 1941: 104.

Eyster, Warren. "Conversations with James Agee." *SoR* 17 (1981): 346–57.

Fabre, Geneviève. "A Bibliography of the Works of James Agee." *BB* 24 (1963–66): 145+.

Farber, Manny. "Star-Gazing for the Middlebrows." *New Leader* 8 Dec. 1958: 14–15. Rpt. as "Nearer My Agee to Thee" in his *Negative Space: Manny Farber on the Movies*. New York: Praeger, 1971. 84–88.

Faris, Wendy. "The Poetics of Pleasure: Expansive Images in *Swann's Way*." *KRQ* 30 (1983): 359–72.

———. "A Point of Order." *Harvard Advocate* 105.4 (1972): 47.

Fiedler, Leslie A. "Encounter with Death." Review of *A Death in the Family*. *New Republic* 9 Dec. 1957: 25–26.

Fields, Pat. "Knoxvillian Nostalgically Recalls Visit with Agee in NY." *Knoxville Journal* 2 Nov. 1962: 8.

Fieschi, J. et al. "Les ecrivans-scenaristes." *Cinematographe* 53 (1979): 54–69.*

Fitzgerald, Robert E., ed. Introduction. *Collected Poems of James Agee*. Boston: Houghton, 1968. ix–xii.

———. "James Agee: A Memoir." *KR* 30 (1968): 587–624. Rpt. in Fitzgerald, ed. *Collected Prose of James Agee*. 1–57; Madden 35–94.

Flanders, Mark Wilson. "Film Theory of James Agee." *DAI* 33 (1973): 3687A–88A. Diss. U of Iowa.

———. *Film Theory of James Agee*. Dissertations on Film Series. New York: Arno, 1977.

Fletcher, Angus. "Dedication to James Agee." *Cambridge Review* 77 (1955–56): 8–11.

Flint, James H. Response to John Updike's 'No Use Talking.' *New Republic* 27 Aug. 1962: 30–31.

Flye, James H. "An Article of Faith." *Harvard Advocate* 105.4 (1972): 15+. Rpt. in Madden 14–22.

————, ed. Preface and Introduction. *Letters of James Agee to Father Flye.*
New York: Braziller, 1962; 2d ed. New York: Houghton, 1971. v–x,
11–13.

————. "Reminiscences and Reflections." *Holy Cross Magazine* 56
(1945): 297–301.

Fortinberry, Alicia. "Let Us Now Remember a Famous Man." *FYI* 3 Feb.
1975: 2ff.

Freeman, James A. "Agee's 'Sunday' Meditation." *CP* 3.2 (1970): 37–39.

Friedman, Lillian H. "A Bookseller's Fall Forecast." *Saturday Review* 12
Oct. 1957: 16–17.

Frohock, W. M. "James Agee: The Question of Unkept Promise." *SWR*
42 (1957): 221–29.

————. "James Agee: The Question of Wasted Talent." *The Novel of
Violence in America.* Boston: Beacon, 1964. 212–30.

Frumkin, Gene. "A Sentimental Foray." *Coastlines* 11 (1958): 53–54.*

Fuller, Edmund. "I'd Do Anything on Earth to Write." Review of *Letters
of James Agee to Father Flye. New York Times Book Review* 22 July 1962:
1+.

Fultz, James R. "A Classic Case of Collaboration: *The African Queen.*"
*LFQ* 10 (1982): 13–24.

————. "Heartbreak at the Blue Motel: James Agee's Scenario of
Stephen Crane's Story." *MQ* 21 (1980): 423–34.

————. "High Jinks at Yellow Sky: James Agee and Stephen Crane."
*LFQ* 11 (1983): 46–54.

————. "James Agee's Film Scripts: Adaptation and Creation." *DAI* 39
(1979): 3884A–85A. Diss. U of Nebraska–Lincoln.

————. "Mr. Agee Himself on Film." *LFQ* 9 (1981): 261–64.

————. "The Poetry and Danger of Childhood: James Agee's Film
Adaptation of *The Night of the Hunter.*" *WHR* 34 (1980): 90–98.

Galloway, David. "The Minor Contemporary Novelist: David Galloway's
*A Family Album.*" *DQR* 12 (1982): 2–14.

Gatlin, Rochelle. "The Personal and Religious Realism of James Agee."
*DAI* 39 (1978): 1679A–80A. Diss. U of Pennsylvania.

Goodman, Paul. Review of *Let Us Now Praise Famous Men. Partisan Review*
9 (1942): 86–87.

Green, David Leslie. "The Modernist American Landscape." *DAI* 43
(1983): 3595A. Diss. Brown U.

Gregory, Charles, and William Dorman. "The Children of James Agee."
*JPC* 9 (1976): 996–1002.

Gregory, Horace. "The Beginning of Wisdom." Review of *Permit Me
Voyage. Poetry* 46 (1935): 48–51.

Griffith, Richard. "Reflections and Images." Review of *Agee on Film* [vol.
1]. *New York Times Book Review* 16 Nov. 1958: 5+.

Grossman, James. "Mr. Agee and The New Yorker." *Partisan Review* 12
(1945): 112–19.

Hammel, William Muller. "James Agee and Motion Pictures." *DAI* 35
(1975): 5568A. Diss. U of Texas–Austin.

Harker, Jonathan. Review of *Agee on Film. Film Quarterly* 12.3 (1959): 58–
61.

Havighurst, Walter. "What Living Is." Review of *A Death in the Family.
Saturday Review* 16 Nov. 1957: 49.

Hayes, Richard. "Rhetoric of Splendor." *Commonweal* 68 (1958): 591–92.

Hersey, John. Introduction. *Let Us Now Praise Famous Men: Three Tenant
Families.* By James Agee and Walker Evans. Boston: Houghton,
1988. v–xl.

Hicks, Granville. "Literary Horizons." Review of *Collected Short Prose of
James Agee. Saturday Review* 1 Mar. 1969: 26.

———. "Suffering Face of the Rural South." Review of *Let Us Now Praise
Famous Men. Saturday Review* 10 Sept. 1960: 19–20.

Hoffman, Frederick J. "James Agee and Flannery O'Connor: The
Religious Consciousness." *The Art of Southern Fiction: A Study of Some
Modern Novelists.* Carbondale: Southern Illinois UP, 1967. 74–95.

Holder, Alan. "Encounter in Alabama: Agee and the Tenant Farmer."
*VQR* 42 (1966): 189–206.

Holland, Norman N. "Agee on Film: Reviewer Re-Viewed." Review of
*Agee on Film* [vol. 1]. *Hudson Review* 12 (1959): 148–51.

Holman, David Marion. "James Agee." *The History of Southern Literature.*
Ed. Louis D. Rubin, et al. Baton Rouge: Louisiana State UP, 1985.
476–78.

Homolka, Florence. "Jim's Many Gestures." Madden 148–52.

Hoopes, James. "Modernist Criticism and Transcendental Literature." *NEQ* 52 (1979): 451–66.

Howes, Victor. "Verse Souvenirs of a Journey into Prose." Review of *Collected Poems of James Agee*. *Christian Science Monitor* 28 Dec. 1968: 9.

Hughes, Riley. Review of *A Death in the Family*. *Catholic World* 186 (1958): 309–10.

Humphreys, David Marshall. "The Aesthetics of Failure: James Agee's Tragic Sensibility." *DAI* 40 (1979): 2681A. Diss. Case Western Reserve U.

Huse, Nacy Lyman. *John Hersey and James Agee: A Reference Guide*. Boston: Hall, 1978.

Hussey, John P. "Agee's Famous Men and American Non-Fiction." *CE* 40 (1979): 677–82.

Huston, John. Foreward. *Agee on Film: Five Film Scripts*. By James Agee. 2 vols. New York: McDowell, 1960. 2: ix–xi. Rpt. in Madden 145–47.

Hynes, Samuel. "James Agee: Let Us Now Praise Famous Men." *Landmarks of American Writing*. Ed. Hennig Cohen. New York: Basic, 1969. 328–40.

"In Love and Anger." Review of *Let Us Now Praise Famous Men*. *Time* 26 Sept. 1960: 112.

Jackson, David. Review of *Collected Short Prose of James Agee*. *Poetry* 114 (1969): 411–12.

Jackson, Katherine Gauss. Review of *Collected Short Prose of James Agee*. *Harpers* Mar. 1969: 109.

"James Agee." *Film Dope* 39 (Mar. 1988): 3–4.*

"James Agee." *Life* 1 Nov. 1963: 57+.

"James Agee." *Twentieth Century Literary Criticism* 1 (1978): 1–19.

"James Agee, 45, Poet and Critic. Obituary. *New York Times* 18 May 1955: 31.

"James (Rufus) Agee." *Twentieth Century Literary Criticism* 19 (1986): 15–49.

Johansen, Ruthann K. "The Sound of Jubilation: Toward an Explication of Agee's Musical Form." *SoQ* 18.2 (1980): 18–31.

Joss, Gerald Alan. "American Film Criticism, 1940–69: A Comparative Study." *DAI* 34 (1974): 4266A. Diss. U of Minnesota.

Kauffmann, Stanley. "A Life in Reviews." Review of *Agee on Film* [vol. 1]. *New Republic* 1 Dec. 1958: 18–19.

Kaufman, Wallace. "Our Unacknowledged Poetry: An Essay on James Agee." *Agenda* 4.3–4 (1966): 68–75.

Kazin, Alfred. "Good-by to James Agee." *Contemporaries.* Boston: Little, 1962. 185–87. Rpt. in *On Contemporary Literature.* Ed. Richard Kostelanetz. New York: Avon, 1969. 222–24.

———. "A Universe of Feeling." Review of *A Death in the Family. New York Times Book Review* 17 Nov. 1957: 5+.

———. "A Wounded Life: A Father 'Perfect in Death.'" *New York Times Book Review* 29 June 1986: 3+.

King, Richard H. "From Theme to Setting: Thomas Wolfe, James Agee, Robert Penn Warren." *A Southern Renaissance: The Cultural Awakening of the American South, 1930–1955.* New York: Oxford UP, 1980. 194–241.

Kirstein, Lincoln. "First Poems." Review of *Permit Me Voyage. New Republic* 27 Feb. 1935: 80–81.

Klug, Michael A. "James Agee and the Furious Angel." *CRevAs* 11 (1980): 313–45.

Knight, Arthur. "Tales of Two Critics." Review of *Agee on Film* [vol. 1]. *Saturday Review* 20 Dec. 1958: 9.

Kramer, Victor A. "Agee and Plans for the Criticism of Popular Culture." *JPC* 5 (1972): 755–66.

———. "Agee: A Study of the Poetry, Prose, and Unpublished Manuscript." *DAI* 30 (1969): 2533A. Diss. U of Texas–Austin.

———. "Agee in the Forties: The Struggle to Be a Writer." *TQ* 11.1 (1968): 9–17.

———. "Agee's Early Poem 'Pygmalion' and His Aesthetic." *MissQ* 29 (1975–76): 191–96.

———. "Agee's *Let Us Now Praise Famous Men*: Images of Tenant Life." *MissQ* 25 (1971–72): 405–17.

————. "Agee's Projected Screenplay for Chaplin: Scientists and Tramps." *SHR* 7 (1973): 357–64.

————. "Agee's Skepticism about Art and Audience." *SoR* 17 (1981): 320–31.

————. "Agee's Use of Regional Material in *A Death in the Family*." *AppalJ* 1 (1972): 72–80.

————. Review of *Collected Poems of James Agee*. *Commonweal* 90 (1969): 211+.

————. "The Complete 'Work' Chapter for James Agee's *Let Us Now Praise Famous Men*." *TQ* 15.2 (1972): 27–48.

————. "The Consciousness of Technique: The Prose Method of James Agee's *Let Us Now Praise Famous Men*." *Literature at the Barricades: The American Writer in the 1930s*. Ed. Ralph F. Bogardus and Fred Hobson. Tuscaloosa: U of Alabama P, 1982. 114–25.

————. "*A Death in the Family* and Agee's Projected Novel." *Proof* 3 (1973): 139–54.

————. "James Agee." *Literature of Tennessee*. Ed. Ray Willbanks. Macon: Mercer UP, 1984. 133–48.

————. *James Agee*. TUSAS 252. Boston: Twayne, 1975.

————. "James Agee Papers at the University of Texas." *LCUT* 8.2 (1966): 33–36.

————. "James Agee's Unpublished Manuscript and His Emphasis on Religious Emotion in *The Morning Watch*." *TSL* 17 (1972): 159–64.

————. "The Manuscript and the Text of James Agee's *A Death in the Family*." *PBSA* 65 (1971): 257–66.

————. "Premonition of Diaster: An Unpublished Section for Agee's *A Death in the Family*." *Costerus* ns 1 (1974): 83–93.

————. "'Religion at Its Deepest Intensity': The Stasis of Agee's *The Morning Watch*." *Renascence* 27 (1975): 221–30.

Kronenberger, Louis. *No Whippings, No Gold Watches*. Boston: Little, 1965. 138–42. Rpt. as "A Real Bohemian." in Madden 108–13.

LaFarge, Oliver. "A Boy Is Risen." Review of *The Morning Watch*. *Saturday Review* 31 Mar. 1951: 18.

Lakin, R. D. "D. W.'s: The Displaced Writer in America." *MQ* 4 (1963): 295–303.

Lamers, William M. "The Absent Father." *Fathering: Fact or Fable.* Ed. Edwards V. Stein. Nashville, TN: Abingdon, 1977.

Larsen, Erling. *James Agee.* UMPAW 95. Minneapolis: U of Minnesota P, 1971.

———. "Let Us Not Now Praise Ourselves." *Carleton Miscellany* 2.1 (1961): 86–97.

Lawbaugh, William M. "'Remembrance of Things Past': An Analysis of James Agee's Prose Style." *DAI* 34 (1973): 1919A. Diss. U of Missouri–Columbia.

Lechlitner, Ruth. "Alabama Tenant Families." Review of *Let Us Now Praise Famous Men. New York Herald Tribune Book Review* 24 Aug. 1941: 10.

Ledbetter, Tony Mark. "Narrative Virtue: A Study of Character in the Works of James Agee, Walker Percy, and Robert Penn Warren." *DAI* 49 (1988): 89A. Diss. Emory U.

Review of *Let Us Now Praise Famous Men. Newsweek* 5 Sept. 1960: 74.

Review of *Let Us Now Praise Famous Men. New Yorker* 13 Sept. 1941: 59–60.

Review of *Letters of James Agee to Father Flye. Booklist* 59 (1962): 20.

Levin, Meyer. "Abraham Lincoln through the Picture Tube." *Reporter* 14 Apr. 1953: 31–33.

Little, Michael V. "Sacramental Realism in James Agee's Major Prose." *DAI* 35 (1974): 2996A–97A. Diss. U of Delaware.

Lum, Albert W. H. "James Agee: The Child as Synthesis." *DAI* 38 (1978): 6727A. Diss. U of Notre Dame.

Macdonald, Dwight. "Agee and the Movies." *Dwight Macdonald on Movies.* Englewood Cliffs, NJ: Prentice, 1969. 3–14.

———. "Death of a Poet." *New Yorker* 16 Nov. 1957: 204+. Rpt. in his *Against the American Grain.* New York: Random, 1962. 143–59; Madden 127–44.

———. "James Agee." *Against the American Grain.* New York: Random, 1962. 159–66. Rpt. in Madden 119–27.

————. "James Agee: Some Memories and Letters." *Encounter* 19.6 (1962): 73–84.

————. "On Chaplin, Verdoux and Agee." *Esquire* Apr. 1965: 18+.

————. "A Way of Death." *Politics Past.* 1957. New York: Viking, 1970. 262–66. [Originally titled *Memoirs of a Revolutionist*].

MacLean, Robert. "Narcissus and the Voyeur: James Agee's *Let Us Now Praise Famous Men.*" *JNT* 11 (1981): 33–52.

————. *Narcissus and the Voyeur: Three Books and Two Films.* New York: Mouton, 1979.

MacLeish, Archibald. Foreward. *Permit Me Voyage.* By James Agee. 1934. New Haven: Yale UP, 1962: 5–7.

Madden, David. "On the Mountain with Agee." *Remembering James Agee.* Ed. David Madden. Baton Rouge: Louisiana State UP, 1974. 1–13.

*Reviews*

Lebowitz, Martin. "Let Us Now Praise. . . . " *New Republic* 12 Apr. 1975: 30.

Levitin, Alexis. Review. *America* 132 (1975): 484–85.

Maddocks, Melvin. "Agee's Last Work." Review of *A Death in the Family. Christian Science Monitor* 14 Nov. 1957: 11.

————. Review of *Letters of James Agee to Father Flye. Christian Science Monitor* 26 July 1962: C7.

Maland, Charles. "Agee: A Film." *SoQ* 19 (1981): 225–28. Rpt. in *The South and Film.* Ed. Warren French. Jackson: UP of Mississippi, 1981. 225–28.

Mann, Charles W. Review of *Agee on Film. Library Journal* 83 (1958): 3509.

————. Review of *Agee on Film,* vol 2. *Library Journal* 85 (1960): 143.

————. Review of *Letters of James Agee to Father Flye. Library Journal* 87 (1962): 2754.

Matthews, T. S. "Agee at Time." *Harvard Advocate* 105.4 (1972): 25–26. Rpt. in Madden 114–18.

————. "James Agee: Strange and Wonderful." *Saturday Review* 16 Apr. 1966: 22–23.

Mayo, Charles W. "James Agee: His Literary Life and Work." *DAI* 30 (1970): 4993A. Diss. George Peabody College.

McClary, Ben Harris. "Sarah Barnwell Elliott's Jerry: An Adolescent Reading Experience Reflected in James Agee's *A Death in the Family.*" *AN&Q* 20 (1982): 113–15.

McCord, David. "Young Poets." Review of *Permit Me Voyage. YR* ns 24 (1935): 391–94.

McDowell, David. "The Turning Point." Madden 95–102.

Mills, C. Wright. "Sociological Poetry." *Politics* 5 (1948): 125–26.

Mills, Moylan. C. "Charles Laughton's Adaptation of *The Night of the Hunter.*" *LFQ* 16 (1988): 49–57.

Milner, Joseph O. "Autonomy and Communion in *A Death in the Family.*" *TSL* 21 (1976): 105–13.

Moore, Roger. "Let Us Now Praise a Famous Author." *Knoxville Journal* 24 Mar. 1989: B1+.

————. "Spears' Film 'Agee' Was 5 Years in the Making." *Knoxville Journal* 24 Mar. 1989: B1+.

Moreau, Geneviève. *The Restless Journey of James Agee.* Trans. Miriam Kleiger and Morty Schiff. New York: Morrow, 1977.

*Reviews*

Matthews, T. S. Review. *New Republic* 16 Apr. 1977: 30–31.

Review. *New Yorker* 18 Apr. 1977: 159–60.

Wilson, Nina K. Review. *Library Journal* 102 (1977): 497.

Wolff, Geoffrey. "Man without Qualities." *New York Times Book Review* 1 May 1977: 56–57.

Morris, Wright. "James Agee." *Earthly Delight, Unearthly Adornments: American Writers as Image-Makers.* New York: Harper, 1978. 155–61.

Morse, Jonathan. "James Agee, Southern Literature and the Domain of Metaphor." *SAQ* 76 (1977): 309–17.

Mosel, Tad. "All the Way Home" [Text of stageplay based on *A Death in the Family*]. *Theatre Arts* Oct. 1962: 25–56.

*Reviews*

"All the Way Home Goes Home." *New York Times Magazine* 11 Nov. 1962: 130–31.

Aston, Frank. "'All the Way Home' Opens at the Belasco." *New York World Telegram* 1 Dec. 1960.

Atkinson, Brooks. Review. *New York Times* 27 Dec. 1960: 26.

"Best U.S. Play of Season." *Life* 27 Jan. 1961: 93.

Brustein, Robert. "Blood and Water." 26 Dec. 1960: 20–21.

Cantor, Arthur. "The Play That Wouldn't Die." *Theatre Arts* June 1961: 64–65.

Chapman, John. "'All the Way Home' Tender, Well Acted, Human, but Unexciting." *Daily News* 1 Dec. 1960.

Clurman, Harold. Review. *Nation* 191 (1960): 49.

Coleman, Robert. "'All Way Home' Misses Mark." *New York Mirror* 1 Dec. 1960.

Duprey, Richard. Review. *Catholic World* 193 (1961): 206–8.

Hayes, Richard. "Honorable Sentiments." *Commonweal* 73 (1960–61): 588.

Hewes, Henry. "Members of the Funeral." *Saturday Review* 17 Dec. 1960: 28–29.

Kerr, Walter. "First Night Report: 'All the Way Home.' *New York Herald Tribune* 1 Dec. 1960.

Lewis, Theophilus. Review. *America* 104 (1961): 546+.

McCarten, John. Review. *New Yorker* 10 Dec. 1960: 96+.

McClain, John. "Tear-Jerker Has High and, Alas, Low Spots." *Journal American* 1 Dec. 1960.

"New Play on Broadway." *Time* 12 Dec. 1960: 76.

"People Are Talking About . . . 'All the Way Home.'" *Vogue* 1 Feb. 1961: 167.

Pryce-Jones, Alan. Review. *Theatre Arts* Feb. 1961: 11.

Taubman, Howard. Review. *New York Times* 18 Dec. 1960, sec. 2: 3.

———. "Theatre: Version of Agee's 'Death in the Family.'" *New York Times* 1 Dec. 1960: 42.

Watts, Richard. "A Striking Drama about Death." *New York Post* 1 Dec. 1960.

Müller, Christopher. "On the Intended Effect of the Narrative Form in James Agee's Book: *Let Us Now Praise Famous Men.*" Wiss-Zeits. der Humboldt-Universitat zu Berlin. Gesellschaftwissenschaftliche Reihe, 1984.*

Murray, Edward. "James Agee: 'Amateur Critic.'" *Nine American Film Critics: A Study of Theory and Practice.* New York: Ungar, 1975. 5–23.

Nelson, Elizabeth. Review of *Collected Poems of James Agee. Library Journal* 93 (1968): 3013.

———. Review of *Collected Short Prose of James Agee. Library Journal* 94 (1969): 550.

Neuman, Alma. "Thoughts of Jim: A Memoir of Frenchtown and James Agee." *Shenandoah* 33.1 (1981–82): 25–36.

Newton, Scott. "David McDowell on James Agee." *WHR* 34 (1980): 117–30.

"Novels and Tates." Review of *The Morning Watch. U.S. Quarterly Book Review* 7 (1951): 144.

Nyren, Dorothy. "James Agee." *A Library of Literary Criticism.* New York: Ungar, 1960. 5–7.

Ohlin, Peter H. *Agee.* New York: Obolensky, 1966.

———. "James Agee: A Critical Study." *DA* 25 (1965): 5284. Diss. U of New Mexico.

Paulding, Gouverneur. "Early on Good Friday." Review of *The Morning Watch. New York Herald Tribune Book Review* 18 Apr. 1951: 14.

Pechter, William. S. "On Agee on Film." *Sight and Sound* 33 (1964): 148–53. Rpt. in *Twenty-Four Times a Second: Films and Film-Makers.* New York: Harper, 1971. 261–75.

Review of *Permit Me Voyage. TLS* 21 Feb. 1935: 111.

"The Perpetual Promise of James Agee." *TLS* 9 June 1972: 659–60.

Perry, J. Douglas. "James Agee and the American Romantic Tradition." *DA* 29 (1968) 1233A. Diss. Temple U.

———. "Thematic Counterpoint in *A Death in the Family*: The Function of the Six Extra Scenes." *Novel* 5 (1972): 234–41.

Phelps, Robert. "The Genius of James Agee." Review of *A Death in the Family. National Review* 7 Dec. 1957: 523–24.

———. "James Agee." Flye, *Letters* 1–10.

———. "Texture of Life." Review of *The Morning Watch. Freeman* 27 Aug. 1951: 767.

Phillipson, John S. "Character, Theme, and Symbol in The Morning Watch." *WHR* 15 (1961): 359–67.

Pickrel, Paul. Review of *A Death in the Family. Harper's Magazine* Dec. 1957: 88.

P[ooke?], C. G. "Poems by James Agee." Review of *Permit Me Voyage. New York Times Book Review* 30 Dec. 1934: 10.

"Portrait." *Saturday Review* 12 Oct. 1957: 16.

"Posthumous and Personal." Review of *A Death in the Family. Newsweek* 18 Nov. 1957: 138–39.

Pratt, Linda Ray. "Imagining Existence: Form and History in Steinbeck and Agee." *SoQ* ns 11 (1975): 84–98.

Presler, Titus. "The Poetry of James Agee." *Harvard Advocate* 105.4 (1972): 35–37.

Pryce-Jones, Alan. Preface. *The Morning Watch.* By James Agee. New York: Ballantine, 1966. vii–xvii.

Raines, Howell. "Let Us Now Revisit Famous Folk." *New York Times Magazine* 25 May 1980: 31+.

Ramsey, Roger. "The Double Structure of The Morning Watch." *SNNTS* 4 (1972): 494–503.

"Rare Legacy of a Poet." *Life* 27 Jan. 1961: 96.

Reed, T. V. "Unimagined Existence and the Fiction of the Real: Postmodernist Realism in *Let Us Now Praise Famous Men.*" *Representations* 24 (1988): 156–76.

Rewak, William J. "James Agee's *Let Us Now Praise Famous Men*: The Shadow over America." *TSL* 21 (1976): 91–104.

———. "James Agee's *The Morning Watch*: Through Darkness to Light." *TQ* 16.3 (1973): 21–37.

———. "The Shadow and the Butterfly: James Agee's Treatment of Death." *DAI* 31 (1970): 2398A. Diss. U of Minnesota.

"Richard's Ordeal." Review of *The Morning Watch. Time* 23 Apr. 1951:
119–20.

Robertson, Priscilla. "Agee's Special View." *Progressive* 25.1 (1961): 44–
45.

Rodman, Seldon. "The Poetry of Poverty." *Saturday Review* 23 Aug.
1941: 6.

Roe, Michael Morris, "A Point of Focus in James Agee's *A Death in the
Family.*" *TCL* 8 (1966): 149–53.

Rolo, Charles. "Of Love and Loss." *Atlantic* 201.1 (1958): 79.

Roud, Richard. "Face to Face: James Agee." *Sight and Sound* 28 (1959):
98–100.

Rubin, Louis D., Jr. "Trouble on the Land: Southern Literature and the
Great Depression." *CRevAs* 10 (1979): 153–74. Rpt. in *Literature at
the Barricades: The American Writer in the 1930s.* Ed Ralph F. Bogardus
and Fred Hobson. Tuscaloosa: U of Alabama P, 1982. 96–113.

Ruhe, Edward. "James Agee." *Epoch* 8 (1957): 247–51.

Ruoff, Gene W. "*A Death in the Family*: Agee's Unfinished Novel." *The
Fifties: Fiction, Poetry, Drama.* Ed. Warren French. Deland, FL:
Everett/Edwards, 1970. 121–32.

Rupp, Richard. "James Agee: The Elegies of Innocence." *Celebration in
Postwar American Fiction, 1945–1967.* Coral Gables: U of Miami P,
1970. 99–111.

Ryan, Nancy Margaret. "James Agee and *Let Us Now Praise Famous Men*:
A Study of Process and Genre." *DAI* 36 (1975): 894A. Diss. U of
Nebraska–Lincoln.

Samway, Patrick. "James Agee: A Family Man." *Thought* 47 (1972): 40–
68.

Saudek, Robert. "J. R. Agee '32 / A Snapshot Album: 1928–1932."
*Harvard Advocate* 105.4 (1972): 18–22. Rpt. in Madden 23–34.

Schoenfeld, Bernard C. "Aiken, Agee, and Sandburg: A Memoir." *VQR*
59 (1983): 299–315.

Schott, Webster. "A Writer Who Began as a Poet." *New York Times Book
Review* 10 Nov. 1968: 63.

Schramm, Richard Robert. "James Agee and the South." *DAI* 40 (1979):
860A. Diss. U of North Carolina–Chapel Hill.

Scott, Winfield Townley. "Agee's Mature and Masterful Last Novel."
*New York Herald Tribune Book Review* 17 Nov. 1957: 3.

———. "Most Famous 'Unknown' Book in Contemporary Letters." *New York Herald Tribune Book Review* 9 Oct. 1960: 6.

———. "When James Agee Went to the Movies." Review of *Agee on Film* [vol. 1]. *New York Herald Tribune Book Review* 15 Feb. 1959: 12.

Seib, Kenneth. *James Agee: Promise and Fulfillment.* Pittsburgh: U of Pittsburgh P, 1968.

———. "Promise and Fulfillment: A Study of James Agee." *DA* 27 (1967): 4231A. Diss. U of Pittsburgh.

Sheed, Wilfred. "All American." Review of *Collected Short Prose of James Agee. NYRB* 22 May 1969: 36–38. Rpt. as "*Collected Short Prose of James Agee*" in his *The Morning After: Selected Essays.* New York: Farrar, 1971. 52–58.

Shepherd, Allen. "'A Sort of Monstrous Grinding Beauty': Reflections on Character and Theme in James Agee's *A Death in the Family.*" *IEY* 14 (1969): 17–24.

Shloss, Carol. "The Privilege of Perception." *VQR* 56 (1980): 596–611.

Silberberg, Elliot David. "The Celluloid Muse: A Critical Study of James Agee." *DAI* 34 (1974): 6662A. Diss. U of Wisconsin.

Simon, John. "Exemplary Failure." *New York Times Book Review* 14 Aug. 1966: 2+.

———. "Let Us Now Praise James Agee." *Midcentury* 15.6 (1959): 17–22.

———. "Preacher Turned Practioner." *Midcentury* 17.27 (1961): 18–21.

Simon, Kate. "The Kneeling Boy." Review of *The Morning Watch. New Republic* 4 June 1951: 21.

Sinclair, Andrew. "The Driven Man." *Spectator* 204 (1965): 762.

Sinyard, Neil. "The Camera Eye of James Agee." *Filming Literature: The Art of Screen Adaptation.* London: Croom Helm, 1986. 83–98.

Smart, Robert Augustin. "An Examination of the Nonfiction Novel: James Agee, Victor Shklovsky, and Norman Mailer." *DAI* 42 (1981): 2662A. Diss. U of Utah.

Snyder, John J, "James Agee: A Study of His Film Criticism." *DAI* 30 (1970): 3477A–78A. Diss. St. John's U.

————. *James Agee: A Study of His Film Criticism.* Dissertations on Film Series. New York: Arno, 1977.

Sosnoski, James J. "Craft and Intention in James Agee's *A Death in the Family.*" *JGE* 20 (1964): 170–83.

Spears, Ross, director. *Agee.* Film. James Agee Film Project, 1979.

*Reviews*

Canby, Vincent. "Film: Life of 'Agee' Opens New Room at the Bleecker." *New York Times* 14 Nov. 1980: C7.

Crowdus, G. "Agee: A Sovereign Prince of the English Language." *Cineaste* 10.3 (1980): 39+.

Flynn, Barbara. "Agee." *Film News* 37.2 (1980): 22+.

Hitchens, Gordon. "Bio-Pic on James Agee, Film Critic." *Variety* 25 July 1979: 39.

[McCarthy, T.?]. "Agee." *Variety* 24 Sept. 1980: 18+.

Sarris, Andrew. "Films in Focus: Hobgoblins of Reality." *Village Voice* 21–27 Jan. 1981: 45.

————. "Regional Filmmaking: The James Agee Film Project." *SoQ* 19.3–4 (1981): 223–25. Rpt. in *The South and Film.* Ed. Warren French. Jackson: UP of Mississippi, 1981.

Spears, Ross, Jude Cassidy, and Robert Coles, eds. *Agee: His Life Remembered.* New York: Holt, 1985.

Spector, Robert. "More Fuel for the Widening Cult of a Tortured, Tragic Talent." Review of *Letters of James Agee to Father Flye. New York Herald Tribune Book Review* 9 Sept. 1962: 6.

Sragow, Michael. "Agee and Film." *Harvard Advocate* 105.4 (1972): 38–41.

Stanford, Donald E. "The Poetry of James Agee: The Art of Recovery." *SoQ* ns 10.2 (1974): xvi–xix.

Staub, Michael Eric. "As Close as You Can Get: Torment, Speech, and Listening in *Let Us Now Praise Famous Men.*" *MissQ* 41 (1988): 147–60.

————. "From Speech to Text: The 1930s Narratives of John Neihardt, Tillie Olsen, and James Agee." *DAI* 48 (1987): 965A. Diss. Brown U.

Stevenson, David L. "Tender Anguish." Review of *A Death in the Family*. *Nation* 185 (1957): 460–61.

Stott, William. *Documentary Expression and Thirties America*. New York: Oxford UP, 1973.

Stringher, Bonalda. "James Agee." *SA* 17 (1971): 211–50.

Sullivan, Richard. "A Boy and His Faith." Review of *The Morning Watch*. *New York Times Book Review* 8 Apr. 1951: 4.

———. "Fine Novel Poses Mysteries of Life and Death." Review of *A Death in the Family*. *Chicago Sunday Tribune* 17 Nov. 1957, sec. 4: 1+.

———. "Letters Reveal Talented and Aging Man." Review of *Letters of James Agee to Father Flye*. *Chicago Sunday Tribune* 5 Aug. 1962, sec. 4: 3.

Taylor, Gordon O. "The Cruel Radiance of What Is: James Agee." *Chapters of Experience: Studies in 20th Century American Autobiography*. New York: St. Martin's, 1983. 66–78; Published in England as *Studies in Modern American Autobiography*. London: Macmillan, 1983.

Taylor, John Russell. Review of *Agee on Film*. *Sight and Sound* 30 (1960–61): 46–47.

"Tender Realist." Review of *A Death in the Family*. *Time* 18 Nov. 1957: 118.

Thomas, Martha Skinner. "James Agee: A Bio-Bibliography." Thesis. U of Tennessee, Knoxville, 1967.

Thompson, Lovell. [Reply to Dwight Macdonald.] *New Yorker* 15 Feb. 1958: 108.

Thompson, Ralph. "Books of the Times." Review of *Let Us Now Praise Famous Men*. *New York Times* 19 Aug. 1941: 19.

Townsend, R. C. "The Possibilities of Field Work." *CE* 34 (1973): 481–99.

Trilling, Lionel. "An American Classic." *Midcentury* 16 (1960): 3–10. Rpt. in his *Speaking of Literature and Society*. Ed. Diana Trilling. New York: Harcourt, 1980.

———. "Greatness with One Fault in It." *KR* 4 (1942): 99–102.

———. "The Story and the Novel." *Griffin* 7 (1958): 4–12.

"The Unquiet One." Review of *Letters of James Agee to Father Flye*. *Time* 3 Aug. 1962: 60.

Untermeyer, Louis, ed. "James Agee." *Modern American Poetry.* New York: Harcourt, 1962: 603.

Updike, John. "No Use Talking." Review of *Letters of James Agee to Father Flye. New Republic* 13 Aug. 1962: 23–24.

von Bragh, P. "Elokuvakritiikin Klassikoita James Agee." *Filmihullu* 6 (1975): 14–18.*

Wagenknecht, Edward. "Films: Few Words and Fine." Review of *Agee on Film* [vol. 1]. *Chicago Sunday Tribune* 16 Nov. 1958, sec. 4: 12.

Walton, Eda Lou. "In the Classical Tradition." Review of *Permit Me Voyage. New York Herald Tribune Book Review* 9 Dec. 1934: 19.

Ward, J. A. *American Silences: The Realism of James Agee, Walker Evans, and Edward Hopper.* Baton Rouge: Louisiana State UP, 1985.

*Review*

Cohen, Milton A. Review. *AL* 58 (1986): 140–41.

———. "*A Death in the Family:* The Importance of Wordlessness." *MFS* 26 (1980–81): 597–611.

———. "James Agee's Aesthetic of Silence: *Let Us Now Praise Famous Men.*" *TSE* 23 (1978): 193–206.

Weales, Gerald. "The Accidents of Compassion." Review of *A Death in the Family. Reporter* 12 Dec. 1957: 42–43.

———. "The Critic in Love." Review of *Agee on Film* [vol. 1]. *Reporter* 25 Dec. 1958: 38–39.

———. "The Film Writer." Review of *Agee on Film,* vol. 2. *Commonweal* 72 (1960): 134–35.

Wensberg, Erik. "Celebration, Adoration and Wonder." Review of *Let Us Now Praise Famous Men. Nation* 191 (1960): 417–18.

———. "I've Been Reading." *Columbia University Forum* 3.3 (1960): 38–42.

———. Review of *Collected Short Prose of James Agee. New York Times Book Review* 2 Mar. 1969: 5.

West, James L. W. "James Agee's Early Tribute to *Tender Is the Night.*" *Fitzgerald/Hemingway Annual 1970.* Ed. Matthew J. Bruccoli and C. E. Frazer Clark. Washington, DC: NCR/Microcard, 1970. 226–27.

"What Agee Found in Alabama." *TLS* 15 July 1965: 598.

Whittier, Gayle. "Belief and Unbelief in *A Death in the Family.*" *Renascence* 31 (1979): 177–92.

Williams, Don. "His Photos Revealed His Soul." *Knoxville News Sentinel* 24 Mar. 1981: B1.

———. "Let Us Now Praise Famous Men." *Knoxville News Sentinel Showtime* 19 Mar. 1989: 3+.

Wilson, Rob. "The Will to Transcendence in Contemporary American Poet, Ai." *CRevAs* 17 (1986): 437–48.

Woodiel, Dale Paul. "The Comic Element in the Works of James Agee." Thesis. U of Tennessee, Knoxville, 1963.

Wrestling, Louise. "The Loving Observer of *One Time, One Place.*" *MissQ* 39 (1985–86): 587–604.

Wyatt, David. "Generating Voice in *A Death in the Family.*" *Prodigal Sons: A Study in Authorship and Authority.* Baltimore: Johns Hopkins UP, 1980. 101–12.

Wydeven, Joseph J. "Photography and Privacy: The Protests of Wright Morris and James Agee." *MQ* 23 (1981): 103–15.

Young, Thomas Daniel. *Tennessee Writers.* Knoxville: U of Tennessee P, 1981.

Young, Vernon. "Film Chronicle." *Hudson Review* 14 (1961): 270–83.

Youra, Steven John. "'Cruel Radiance': James Agee and the Problems of Portraiture." *DAI* 43 (1983): 3915A. Diss. Cornell U.

———. "James Agee on Films and the Theater of War." *FilmC* 10 (1985): 18–31.

Zaller, Robert. "Let Us Now Praise James Agee." *SLJ* 10.2 (1978): 144–54.

# Contributors

PAUL G. ASHDOWN, professor of journalism at the University of Tennessee, has lectured extensively on James Agee and is the author of *James Agee: Selected Journalism* (University of Tennessee Press, 1985).

EUGENE T. CARROLL, a teacher and counselor with a special background in music, is a longtime Agee devotee who has published on the use of imagery in *A Death in the Family*. He is in private practice in Billings, Montana.

WILMA DYKEMAN, Tennessee state historian and adjunct professor at the University of Tennessee, is the author of many novels and works of nonfiction. Among those published by Holt, Rinehart, and Winston are *The Tall Woman* (1962), *The Far Family* (1966), *Return the Innocent Earth* (1973), and *Too Many People, Too Little Love* (1974). Other nonfiction includes *Seeds of Southern Change* with James Stokely (University of Chicago Press,1962), *Tennessee: A Bicentennial History* (Norton, 1975), and *Explorations* (Wakestone Books, 1984).

VICTOR A. KRAMER, widely known as an authority on James Agee, is professor of English at Georgia State University. Among his works are sixteen articles on Agee, and the books *James Agee* (Twayne, 1975), *Agee and Actuality: Artistic Vision in His Work* (Whitston, 1991), and *Agee: Selected Literary Documents* (University of Tennessee Press, forthcoming). He has also published books about Thomas Merton and Walker Percy and is the founding editor of *The Merton Annual* (AMS Press).

MICHAEL A. LOFARO is the editor of three books on Davy Crockett for the University of Tennessee Press: *Davy Crockett: The Man, the Legend, the Legacy, 1786–1986* (1985), *The Tall Tales of Davy Crockett: The Second Nashville Series of Crockett Almanacs, 1839–1841* (1987), and *Crockett at Two Hundred: New Perspectives on the Man and the Myth* (1989). He is also the author of *The Life and Adventures of Daniel Boone* (University Press of Kentucky, 1978, second revised edition, 1986). Dr. Lofaro is director of graduate studies and professor of English at the University of Tennessee, Knoxville.

DAVID MADDEN is writer-in-residence at Louisiana State University. Among his more than thirty books of fiction and nonfiction are *Remembering James Agee* (Louisiana State University Press, 1974), *Classics of Civil War Fiction*, edited with Peggy Bach (University Press of Mississippi, 1991), and the novel *Bijou* (Crown, 1974). Among his works in progress are *Rediscoveries III: Nonfiction*, edited with Peggy Bach, and *Sharpshooter*, a Civil War novel.

MARY MOSS is a doctoral candidate in the Department of English at the University of Tennessee, Knoxville. She is the author of "An Annotated Bibliography of Agee Criticism."

KATHRYN BLACK SWAIN is a doctoral candidate in the Department of English at the University of Tennessee, Knoxville, where she is completing her dissertation on women, "home," and self-definition in recent novels by American women.

GEORGE BROWN TINDALL, one of the most eminent of southern historians, is the Kenan Professor Emeritus of History at the University of North Carolina at Chapel Hill. Among his extensive publications are three books for the Louisiana State University Press: *The Emergence of the New South, 1913–1945* (volume 10 of *A History of the South*, 1967); *The Persistent Tradition in New South Politics* (1975); and *The Ethnic Southerners* (1976). Other works include *The Disruption of the Solid South* (University of Georgia Press, 1972), and *America: A Narrative History* (Norton, 1984).

LINDA WAGNER-MARTIN has published many books on modern American literary figures such as William Faulkner, William Carlos Williams, T. S. Eliot, Robert Frost, Phyllis McGinley, Ernest Hemingway, Ellen Glasgow, John Dos Passos, Denise Levertov, Joyce Carol Oates, and Anne Sexton. Among her most recent studies are *Sylvia Plath: A Biography* (Simon and Schuster, 1987) and *The Modern American Novel* (Twayne, 1989). She is Hanes Professor of English at the University of North Carolina at Chapel Hill.

# Index

*James Agee: Reconsiderations* was designed by Kay Jursik, composed by The University of Tennessee Press on the Apple ® Macintosh™ SE using Microsoft ® Word and Aldus Pagemaker ®, and printed by Cushing Malloy, Inc. This book is set in New Baskerville and is printed on 50 lb. Glatfelter Natural.